THE MURDERER NEXT DOOR

To his neighbors, Jerry Brudos was a gentle, quiet man whose mild manner sharply contrasted with his awesome physical strength.

To his employers, Jerry was an expert electrician, the kind of skilled worker you just don't find anymore.

To his wife, Darcie, Jerry was a good husband, and a loving father to their children, despite his increasingly bizarre sexual demands on her, and his violent insistence that she never venture into his garage workroom and the giant food freezer there.

To the Oregon police, Jerry Brudos was the most hideously twisted killer they had ever unmasked. And they brought to light what he had done to four young women—and perhaps many more—in the nightmare darkness of his sexual hunger and rage. First, Jerry Brudos was brought to trial . . . and then, in a shattering aftermath, his wife was accused as well. . . .

ANN RULE is a former policewoman who has worked as a true-crime writer for many years, with articles in a host of magazines. In addition, she has lectured widely to law-enforcement schools and agencies. She is regarded as one of the nation's foremost experts on the subject of serial murders. Her bestselling books, *The Want-Ad Killer, The Stranger Beside Me, Possession,* and *Small Sacrifices* are available in Signet editions.

LUST KILLER

ANN RULE
(writing as Andy Stack)

UPDATED EDITION

A SIGNET BOOK

SIGNET
Published by the Penguin Group
Penguin Books USA Inc., 375 Hudson Street,
New York, New York 10014, U.S.A.
Penguin Books Ltd, 27 Wrights Lane,
London W8 5TZ, England
Penguin Books Australia Ltd, Ringwood,
Victoria, Australia
Penguin Books Canada Ltd, 10 Alcorn Avenue,
Toronto, Ontario, Canada M4V 3B2
Penguin Books (N.Z.) Ltd, 182–190 Wairau Road,
Auckland 10, New Zealand

Penguin Books Ltd, Registered Offices:
Harmondsworth, Middlesex, England

Published by Signet, an imprint of Dutton Signet,
a division of Penguin Books USA Inc.

First Printing, June, 1983
Fourth Signet Printing (First Printing, Updated Edition,) August, 1988
21 20 19 18 17 16 15

 REGISTERED TRADEMARK—MARCA REGISTRADA

Printed in the United States of America

This book is dedicated to the late Albert Govoni, editor of *True Detective*, with gratitude for fourteen years of friendship and superior editing in crime writing.

Acknowledgements

I wish to thank a number of people and organizations who have helped with the research on this book, and who have shared their memories, reliving the emotions they felt. Although the subject matter is horrific, the book is presented in the hope that it may add to the psychiatric research that may one day find a way to treat aberrant minds before they explode into violence. Barring that, *Lust Killer* is written in the belief that the more we learn about the serial killers who rove America, the more quickly we will stop them from ever killing again.

My gratitude goes to: Lieutenant James Stovall, Salem, Oregon Police Department; Detective Jerry Frazier, Salem Police Department; Lieutenant Gene Daugherty, Oregon State Police Criminal Investigation Unit; Sergeant Rod Englert, Multnomah County, Oregon Department of Public Safety; Detectives B.J. Miller and "Frenchie" De Lamere, Corvallis, Oregon Police Department; Archives Department of the Oregon State Supreme Court; Special Agents John Henry Campbell, R. Roy Hazelwood, John Douglas, and Robert Ressler, of the Federal Bureau of Investigation's Behavioral Science Unit, Quantico, Virginia.

Special thanks to Sharon Wood, who survived to relate a terrifying encounter. Most of all, it is my profound hope that some intelligence gained herein will mean that Linda Slawson, Jan Whitney, Karen Sprinker, and Linda Salee did not die in vain, and that understanding their tragedies may save young women old enough to be the daughters they never had.

Prologue

She bent her head against the blast of rain-drenched wind and shifted the heavy case she carried to her other hand. It was January 26, 1968. She was nineteen years old, pretty, slender, and . . . discouraged. Selling encyclopedias door-to-door was not the glorious career her area instructor had promised. It was difficult and scarcely rewarding. Every morning she left her home in Aloha, Oregon—a suburb of Portland—full of enthusiasm, and every evening she returned with her sales book empty. She knew that if she could sell just one set with the yearbooks and the atlas and all the frills that went with it, she would be able to pay rent for a month, buy groceries, and maybe even a few new clothes. That was what kept her going—thinking that each day would be the day. She had listened to the enthusiastic teachers who gave the indoctrination, and she'd memorized all their suggested spiels. She'd even practiced in front of her bedroom mirror, but her prospective customers hadn't reacted the way the role-playing "customers" had in class.

When she knocked on doors, people listened impatiently and then shook their heads and shut the door in her face. When she was given a lead, she usually found that the customer wasn't nearly as interested as she'd been led to believe. Most of them didn't have one book of any kind displayed in their homes, and she couldn't believe they were going to shell out several hundred dollars for a whole set of genuine leather-bound encyclopedias. The best pitch was supposed to be that encyclopedias would make their children succeed in school and grow up to be doctors and lawyers and professors, but it always bothered her to stress the

9

"guilt" approach. "Don't you want your children to have all the advantages you never had? Concerned parents *all* buy encyclopedias for their families, you know."

It bothered her to sit on couches so worn that their bare spots were covered with quilts or towels and suggest that the answer to being poor was to buy her product. She could see the people felt bad enough as it was. She knew if they signed up, they'd be stuck with payments for her fancy books for years. Well, nobody bought anyway, but she always left thinking she'd made them feel worse about being low on money.

The well-to-do homes she approached already had encyclopedias. And those people made *her* feel bad.

Linda Slawson had come from Rochester, Minnesota, to live in Aloha. She had somehow expected warm, balmy weather in Aloha. She had thought of Hawaii and California when she pictured the West Coast and Oregon. Boy, had she been wrong. It rained so much in Portland that it seemed like she never got dry. Sometimes it just drizzled and sometimes it poured and sometimes it blew in soppy gusts—but it always rained. Locals said it got better in the summer, and she should really go into Portland for the Rose Festival in June, but . . .

Her feet hurt. She never should have worn high heels, but she had figured she wouldn't have far to walk from the bus to the address the company had given her near Forty-seventh and Hawthorne. She liked to dress nicely; it made a better impression on customers. But high heels on a darkening rainy night had been a really dumb choice.

Her hands felt numb from carrying the satchel full of heavy books, and she thought the weight of it was what was bothering her neck. When she finally got back to her apartment in Aloha, she was going to have a good hot bath and just forget all about encyclopedias.

She paused under the streetlight, set her gear down, and reached into her purse for the slip of paper with the address on it. The ink smeared instantly in the rain and she couldn't tell if she was supposed to go to 1541 or 1551—or maybe it was 1451. She was tempted to just pack it in, wait for the next bus, and go home.

Indecisive, she started walking again. And then she saw a man in the yard of a house a little way up the block. Maybe she was in luck. He was looking at her, and he waved as if he was expecting someone.

She smiled at him. "I had an appointment to show some encyclopedias to someone. Could this be the house?"

He smiled back and beckoned her in. He was a big man, pudgy but not fat, and he had a moon face. "Come on in."

"Oh, that's good. I thought I was really lost." She moved toward the front steps, but the man took her elbow and pulled her with him, heading to the back.

"There's some company upstairs. We can talk without being interrupted downstairs. My workshop is down there. I'm really interested in buying encyclopcdias. You don't mind?"

She looked at him and debated. He was big, but he looked harmless. Kind of dumb, almost—but he seemed serious about buying, and that hadn't happened in a long time. "Well . . ."

"My mother and my little girl are upstairs, and they have visitors. It would be so noisy. And I want to hear what you have to say."

"Okay. Sure."

She followed him into the basement through a rear door and sat on the stool he pulled up for her. She could hear footsteps overhead, the floor above her creaking.

"So," he said. "Tell me about your encyclopedias. Could I buy them tonight?"

"You could order them. I could get the whole set out to you in . . . say, a week. If you have a little girl, I think you'll be interested in our children's books, too. How old is she?"

He seemed distracted, impatient now. "Oh . . . she's only six—but she's very smart. She's starting to read."

"Good. Here, let me show you . . ." She bent to open the case with her brochures and the sample books.

"Let me turn that light on." He moved behind her. She heard him fumbling with something, and half-turned.

The last thing Linda Slawson felt was a crash against

her head. She fell heavily from the stool, brilliant lights exploding behind her eyes, her ears ringing, and then black velvet covered everything.

He was breathing heavily, although it had taken so little effort to swing the length of two-by-four against her head and feel the satisfying "thunk" when it hit. She had dropped like a stone.

He knelt beside her and checked to see if she was still breathing. He thought he detected a slight movement in her ribs. And then he placed both his hands around her neck and squeezed for a long time. Her neck was so frail; he could feel little bones inside crushing under his hands. When he was sure she was really dead, he let go and stared down at her.

He felt such exhilaration. He had planned and fantasized about doing this for so long. He had come close so many times. Now he had done it, and she belonged to him to do with what he wanted.

He didn't like her hair. It was short—so short that she almost looked like a little boy. He would have preferred a woman with long, flowing hair. Someone who looked like the pictures he'd collected. No matter, really, though, because she had a nice body and she was wearing high heels—the kind he liked.

Footsteps sounded overhead, and he jumped, startled. He wouldn't be able to do all the things he wanted to do if his stupid mother decided to come down and interrupt him. *Damn her.* He'd always hated his mother, and now she had to be here when everything else was going so well.

He worked at quieting his breathing, pulled himself together, and walked upstairs. His mother was there, playing with his daughter. She'd never taken very good care of him, but now she was sure happy to come over and baby-sit. And his wife was always wanting to get away from him, so she just welcomed the old bat every time she showed up.

"I'm starved," he said. "Don't bother with dinner, though. Why don't you take the kid and go get some hamburgers?"

"It's raining. It's nasty out there. Why don't I just fix some—"

He peeled a five-dollar bill out of his wallet, ignoring her dithering. "I want a double-cheeseburger. You get what you want for you two. Stay there and eat yours, and then order mine when you're ready to come home. No hurry. Knock on the floor when you get back."

When they were finally gone, he hurried back to the basement. The girl was still there, still lying just as he had left her. He was so excited, he hardly knew where to start.

But just as he bent over her, he heard someone upstairs again. *Damn!* The steps were heavy male footsteps, and he heard someone shouting his name. Hurriedly he grabbed the body under the arms and dragged it to the shadowy place under the steps. He kicked the satchel full of books into a corner. Then he went out the back door and around the house to the front door. His friend Ned Rawls was there. All happy and glad to see him and walking in like he owned the place. He never should have let Rawls have a key to the place.

He had to make small talk with Ned, and be careful not to show impatience. There was so little time before his mother came home with the kid, or his wife and the new baby came back. He laughed at some joke Ned told him. He explained he had a project in his workshop he had to finish, and promised to call Ned later. It took ten minutes to ease the guy off the porch and back into his car.

When he got back downstairs, he was trembling with anticipation. He pulled the girl out from under the steps. She looked so pale. Normal, as if she was still alive—and that was good—but so pale. Like a big doll. His to play with.

Her skirt and blouse weren't very interesting. He liked pretty clothes, and hers didn't do anything at all for him.

But he had a pleasant surprise when he undressed her. Despite her boy's haircut and plain clothing, she was wearing wonderful underwear. A blue bra and slip and girdle, and beneath the girdle, bright red panties. They were perfect; he couldn't have picked better himself.

He looked at the underclothing and touched it, and removed the garments one by one, especially pleased with the red panties. He redressed her in her fancy bra and slip and girdle, carefully hooking all the hooks. He was good at that. He'd practiced so many times.

He had a long time to play with her before his mother came home with the hamburger for him—but he was frustrated when she rapped on the floor. He had to go up and get the damned thing, thank her, and sit there and eat it as if he was hungry. And all the time, *she* was waiting patiently for him in the basement. He smiled to himself. At least *she* wouldn't go away and leave him, not until he chose to let her go.

When he went back to her, she sat where he'd propped her. He thought about having sex with her, and decided that wasn't necessary. He berated himself because he had no film for his camera. That was an important thing that he'd neglected to do. But he'd had no idea he would meet a door-to-door saleslady and it would be so easy to lie to her and coax her inside.

But he did have all his other precious things. All the filmy, lacy panties and bras that he'd stolen over a long time. He could never decide which was the best— sneaking into dark apartments and stealing the underwear while he could hear the women sighing in their sleep only a few feet away from him, or playing with his collection of satin and silk that still smelled faintly of their perfume and skin after the garments belonged to him.

He'd never had anyone he could use as a model before. He couldn't show all that stuff to his wife, because she might get suspicious. Now he chose bras and panties and slips with inches of lace edging the satin, and spent hours dressing and undressing the girl. He liked the red panties best of all. They were just right for her.

He had worked through the scenarios in his head for years, and never told anyone what he thought of, always dreaming of captive women. And he wasn't disappointed at all now that he had pulled it off. He knew he couldn't keep her with him forever, but he could remember the way it was now. Next time, he would take pictures too.

His wife came home, and he went upstairs and talked to her briefly, and told her to go to bed—he'd be along when he finished his project. He loved his wife. He really did love her, because she was sweet most of the time, and quiet, and because she didn't nag him. But things just weren't the same since the baby boy was born. He'd wanted to be with her when that happened, right there in the delivery room, and she'd chosen to share that experience with another man. With the doctor—not with him. It just tore hell out of him that she'd choose another man like that.

When they were all asleep, he went back to the basement. He played dress-up with the dead girl some more, reveling in the quiet that was marred only by the soft whisper of the rain against the windows. He would have to get rid of her before the sun came up. Too bad, but that's the way it was. He needed to have something that belonged to her, though. Not her bra and panties; he already had so many of those from so many women who didn't even know what he looked like or who had stolen from them.

He had a freezer, but it wasn't big enough to keep her in, and all the women roaming through the house would find her anyway. His mind was working well. He understood certain things clearly. He was right-handed, so it seemed proper that he should cut off her left foot . . ..

He did that, cutting cleanly through her ankle. The foot didn't look right without a shoe, so he slipped the shoe on it before he put the foot into his freezer.

He was pleased with himself. He had convinced Ned Rawls that he was brewing nitroglycerin in the basement, and scared him off easily enough. He'd gotten his fool mother and his wife to go to bed, and now all he had to do was to slip the dead girl into the Willamette River, where no one would ever find her. He already had an engine head to use as a weight, and he was so strong he could handle it easily.

There were many bridges crisscrossing the Willamette River in Portland. In the daytime, cars choked them. But not at two A.M. He chose the St. John Bridge, and just to be on the safe side, he pretended that he had a flat tire. The stupid cops never showed up to help when you really needed them, and he counted on that now. He pulled a jack out of the trunk, nudging her body aside, and set it up under the rear bumper.

It worked like a charm. Nobody in the few cars that passed by even looked twice at him. When there were no cars in sight at all, he lifted the girl from the trunk, along with the engine head, and carried her to the bridge rail. She fell free, and an instant later the deep waters of the Willamette pulled her in and covered her over. The splash itself had been surprisingly gentle, too soft to draw attention.

After he couldn't see her any longer, he undid the car jack, stowed it in the trunk, and drove away. The only thing that bothered him was that he remembered too late the ring she'd worn. Some kind of bulky class ring that said "St. Somebody" on it, and "1967."

He didn't even know her name. It didn't matter. He was sure no one would ever find her.

No one did.

Back at the encyclopedia sales office, they figured that Linda K. Slawson had just decided to quit. Nobody remembered the place where she was supposed to go on the night of January 26. Salespeople came and went. It was to be expected.

Her family worried, and then grew frantic, and made a Missing Persons report to the Portland Police Department. But all efforts of the Missing Persons detectives led nowhere. Linda K. Slawson remained on the missing rolls, certainly not forgotten by either the investigators or by her family. There simply was no place left to look for her. The earth might as well have opened up and swallowed her.

The big man with the moon face kept her foot for a while. He used it as a model to try shoes on. When he grew tired of that game, he put a weight o. tossed it too into the Willamette.

And then he planned and fantasized and wond. what he could do next. What he'd done to the gir. the red panties had been so exciting and so fulfilling that he had no intention of stopping.

1

He was a monster. He was not born a monster, but evolved grotesquely over the twenty-eight years, eleven months, and twenty-seven days that passed before Linda K. Slawson had the great misfortune to cross his path.

Jerome Henry Brudos was born in Webster, South Dakota, on January 31, 1939. His parents seem to have been a hopelessly mismatched couple. They already had one son a few years older than Jerome, and they apparently did not particularly want another; the older brother, Larry, was intelligent and placid and gave them little trouble. A girl would have been preferable. Instead, Eileen Brudos gave birth to a red-haired, blue-eyed second son whom she would never really like. As all babies do, he must have sensed that. When he was old enough to form his feelings into words, he would call her a "stubborn, selfish egotist." If she did not like him, he grew to *despise* her.

Eileen Brudos was a stolid woman who dressed neatly and plainly, and "never, never wore high heels," according to Jerome.

Henry Brudos was a small man—only five feet, four inches tall. He moved his family a dozen times during his sons' growing-up years. They usually lived on a farm, farms that gave so grudgingly of their produce and livestock that the elder Brudos had to work a full-time job in town to support them. Like most small men, Jerry Brudos' father was easily offended and hostile if he thought someone was taking advantage of him, and was quick to react with verbal abuse. Whatever his father's faults, Jerome Brudos vastly preferred him to Eileen Brudos.

The Brudoses lived in Portland during the Second

18

World War. Employment was easy then, ... financial picture was fairly stable.

Five-year-old Jerry Brudos was allowed to ... freely, and on one occasion he was pawing through ... junkyard when he found something that fascinated him. Shoes. Women's high-heeled shoes, but nothing at all like anything his mother had ever worn. These were constructed of shiny patent leather with open toes and open heels and thin straps to encircle the ankles of the woman who wore them. They were a little worn, of course, and one rhinestone-studded decorative clip was missing. Still, they pleased him, and he carried them home.

More for comic effect than anything else, he slipped his stocking feet into the shiny black shoes and paraded around. Eileen Brudos caught him at it and was outraged. She scolded him severely, her voice rising in a shriek as she went on and on about how wicked he was. She ordered him to take the shoes back to the dump and leave them there. He did not understand why she was so angry, or just what it was that he had done wrong—since obviously no one wanted the old shoes anyway. He didn't take the shoes back; instead he hid them. When he was discovered still sashaying around in his forbidden high heels, there was hell to pay. His mother burned the shoes and made him stay in his room for a long time.

When he was finally let out, he ran to a neighbor woman who was very pretty and soft and kind to him. He liked to pretend that she was his real mother and that he had no connection to Eileen. He already hated Eileen.

Little Jerry Brudos had another friend when he was five—a girl his own age. She was often pale and tired and couldn't play; he did not know that she was dying of tuberculosis. Her death was the most terrible thing that had ever happened to him, and he grieved for her for a long time.

The neighbor woman who was kind to him was sickly too, and suffered from diabetes. Years later, in his own mind, the episode with the stolen shoes, his girlfriend's death at the age of five, and the kind

20 oor woman were intertwined in his mind, and he ald not speak of one without the others.

By the time Jerry Brudos was in the first grade, the family had moved to Riverton, California. He had a pretty teacher who invariably wore high-heeled shoes to class. She always had two pairs on hand, one to switch to if her feet got tired or if she planned to go out on a date when school was over. Stealthily now, because he had learned that high-heeled shoes were not to be noticed overtly, he stared at his teacher's footwear, entranced by the slim heels. When he could stand the temptation no longer, he stole the shoes she kept in her desk and hid them under blocks in the play area so he could take them home with him. But somebody found them and took them back to the teacher. Days later, he confessed that he had taken them.

She was more puzzled than angry. "Why on earth would you want my shoes, Jerome?"

He turned red and ran from the room.

Jerry Brudos failed the second grade. He was a sickly child. He had measles and recurring sore throats, accompanied by swollen glands and laryngitis. As an adult he remembered having a number of "toe and finger operations," probably to treat fungus infections around the nails. He had two operations on his legs. What the defect was is obscure; Jerry Brudos himself recalls only that there was something wrong with the veins in his legs: "The veins were ballooning and I had to have the operations because they were not doing their job."

He often had migraine headaches that blinded him with pain and made him vomit. Because of the headaches and because he seemed not to comprehend the basics of reading and writing, school authorities thought he might need glasses. His brother had sailed through school with As, and Jerry's I.Q. tested normal or above, but he sometimes seemed vague and slow.

Glasses were prescribed but they were hardly more than window glass, a placebo. He still had headaches, an ailment that would plague Jerry Brudos to greater and lesser degree for much of his life.

He must have spent some time in bed recovering,

locked in with the mother he avoided whenever possible, but that part of his life is blanked out in his memory.

He got along all right with his brother, despite the fact that Larry excelled in school and was always deferred to by Eileen. Jerry seldom saw his father because he was always working—on the farm or on his town job.

Jerry's fixation with women's shoes was solidly entrenched. On one occasion his parents entertained visitors who brought their teenage daughter with them. The girl wanted to take a nap, and lay down on Jerry's bed. He crept in and was transfixed to see that she still wore her high-heeled shoes. As she slept, one of the heels poked through the loose weave of the blanket. The sight was tremendously erotic to Jerry. He wanted her shoes. He worked to pry them off her feet, but she woke up and told him to stop it and get out of the room.

It should be pointed out that Jerry Brudos was still a small boy when his shoe-stealing episodes took place, well under the age of puberty. Sex, of course, was a subject forbidden in his home. Like all farm-raised youngsters, he observed sexual behavior among animals. He knew what bulls did to cows, and he knew that boars quite literally "screwed" female pigs with their peculiar but functional penises. He had seen dogs and cats mate. But he would never dare to ask how intercourse between humans was accomplished. Touching and hugging, any demonstration of affection, was discouraged in the Brudos home. He heard jokes at school, and laughed with the other boys—remembering particularly a joke about a girl sliding down a banister—but he never admitted he didn't understand the punch line or the point of the joke. And he was completely unable to make the connection between the strange excitement he had when he was around women's shoes and his own sexual drives.

It was just something that was peculiar to himself. But he sensed that it had to be a secret thing. Why else would his mother have been so enraged over his shoe theft when he was only five? Why else would the teenage visitor have been so angry with him? And his very need for subterfuge and secrecy made his obsession all the more thrilling.

Looking at the fair, bland-faced Jerry, the child who seemed dull in school, no one ever detected the fires burning in him. That there was danger there, however incipient, would have seemed laughable.

For all of his life, women held the reins of power over Jerry Brudos—in one way or another. Eileen, his mother, was strong, rigid, and intractable. He could not please her; he had never been able to please her, and she clearly ran the household. She railed at him for the most minor lapses, and it seemed to Jerry that his brother got away with everything. Larry avoided chores just as much as Jerry did, but their mother always had an excuse for Larry. Larry was "exceptional" and "gifted" and needed the time to study. Their father and Larry both knew that Eileen had it in for Jerry, but there was nothing they could do about it. She ruled with a firm hand, and all three males in the family chose evasive tactics rather than confrontation.

The other females who had been important to Jerry Brudos deserted him; his little girlfriend died and left him, the neighbor lady became too ill to have time for him, and his teacher never quite trusted him after he admitted the theft of her shoes. He learned early that women could not be counted on.

He wavered constantly between depression and frustration and the rage that is born of impotence.

Heading into puberty, he was an accident looking for a place to happen.

The family moved to Grants Pass, Oregon. Their new neighbors had a house full of daughters, and Jerry and one of their brothers often sneaked into the girls' bedrooms to play with their clothing. His fetish expanded to include female undergarments. Secret woman things. Brassieres and panties and girdles and the complicated harnesses that they used to hold up their silky nylons. He now loved the feel of the soft cloth, almost as much as the shoes that were so different from men's.

The Brudoses moved again before Jerry was thirteen, and lived on Wallace Pond near Salem, the state capital. Jerry's father made another lackluster attempt at farming there in 1952.

Larry was sixteen and had the normal pubescent male's interest in the nude female body. He collected pinup pictures and sometimes drew pictures of Superman's girlfriend, Lois Lane—portraying Lois nude and wearing high heels. Given the puritanical views of Eileen Brudos, Larry prudently kept his cache of pictures locked up in a box.

Jerry found the box, picked the lock, and pored over the pictures. And it was Jerry—not Larry—who was caught in the act. He didn't tell on his brother, but accepted the punishment. Nobody would have believed that it was Larry's collection anyway, because Larry was the good son and Jerry was the bad son.

At the age of sixteen, Jerry had his first wet dream. Eileen, who steadfastly denied all sexual matters, found his stained sheets and scolded him severely. The nocturnal ejaculation had startled him, too, and he wondered if it was something people should be able to control. His mother made him wash his sheets by hand, and he had to sleep without sheets the next night because he had only one set and the offending sheets were still hanging damp on the line.

Jerry began to create bizarre fantasies of revenge. He worked for days digging a hidden tunnel in the side of a hill on the farm. His plan was to get a girl and put her into the tunnel. Once he had her, he would make her do anything he wanted. He could picture it all clearly, but he ran into a problem when he tried to think what it was he wanted the captive girl to do. He still didn't know enough about sex to focus on what intercourse was, and he certainly didn't understand rape. He only knew that the thought of a captive woman begging for mercy excited him.

At the same time, Jerry began to steal shoes and undergarments from neighbors' houses and clotheslines. He had quite a little stash that he studied and touched and kept carefully away from Eileen Brudos.

Interestingly, Jerry never stole his mother's clothing or was tempted to try her things on.

If anyone suspected that it was Jerry who was making off with the neighborhood underwear on Wallace Pond, he was never accused. And then the peripatetic Brudoses moved again—this time to Corvallis. Corvallis is the site of Oregon State University and lies twenty-five miles west of what is today the I-5 freeway that runs from Canada to Mexico. It is a fertile region, as is the entire Willamette Valley. The Long Tom River flows just east of Corvallis, and the Pacific Ocean is fifty miles to the west.

By the time the family moved onto yet another farm, Larry was in college—doing well in his study of electronics. Jerry was skilled in the same field, but his accomplishments paled in comparison to his brother's.

Jerry was almost seventeen, and he had learned the basic facts of life. Still, he had never *seen* a naked woman, and he was determined that he would. His hostility toward and distrust of women in no way mitigated his lusting after them.

Jerry continued to steal women's clothing. At home, in the privacy of his own room, he would take his treasures from their hiding spot and fondle them. He would later tell psychiatrists that touching female garments gave him "a funny feeling." He used the clothing for masturbation, but he failed to achieve an orgasm. The only ejaculation he had experienced to date had come from "wet dreams."

In the late summer of 1955, Jerry Brudos crept into a neighbor's house and stole undergarments belonging to an eighteen-year-old girl who lived there. The stolen clothing by itself soon began to pall, and Jerry thought that it would be so much better if he could have pictures of a real girl, mementos he could keep. He formulated a complicated scheme.

He approached the girl whose lingerie he'd stolen and told her that he could help her get her things back. He bragged to her about a secret; he had been working with the police on the case. He had inside information. She was a little doubtful, but Jerry was persuasive. Since he lived in the neighborhood where the thefts had occurred, he said the police found him the perfect undercover man—no one would suspect he was working with the cops.

The girl debated. She wanted her things back; she'd worked hard to buy them. And Jerry was a kid—only sixteen; he looked like a big clown. She wasn't afraid of him, and maybe he *did* know something.

Jerry Brudos invited her to his home on a night when he knew everyone else in his family would be gone. When he heard her knock on the door, he called to her from upstairs, "Up here! Come on up—"

She edged up the shadowy staircase of the old farmhouse, following the sound of his voice. His room was dim and she couldn't see Jerry. Suddenly, a tall figure wearing a mask jumped out at her and waved a large knife.

"Take off your clothes—or I'll cut you," the voice behind the mask said. "Do it!"

He pressed the knife against her throat, and she could feel its sharp edge cutting. Her heart convulsed as she realized she had made a terrible mistake in judgment.

Trembling, the girl removed her clothing. She wasn't stupid; she knew who it was behind the mask—but she didn't know what he was going to do to her. She didn't have a chance to fight, she'd have to go along with him.

Her captor produced a cheap camera with a flash attachment, and she realized that he wasn't going to rape her; he wanted to take pictures of her!

He directed her how to pose, and took some shots when she was totally naked, and then some when she was partially clothed. She did what he asked, terrified that he might still have more in mind than photographs. He moved quickly, giving her orders to move this way, to bend, to turn.

When the roll of film was finished, the masked figure walked out of Jerry Brudos' bedroom. His victim threw on the rest of her clothes frantically and was just heading toward the stairs when Jerry, without a mask, walked into his bedroom. He was breathing heavily.

"Hey, are you OK?" he asked. "I was out in the barn, and somebody came along—I couldn't see who it was—and locked me in. I just managed to break out! Did you see anyone around here?"

She shook her head, and edged past him, running for home the minute she made it to the front door.

Jerry Brudos actually believed he'd fooled his victim into believing it was a stranger who had forced her to pose nude. He figured he'd pulled it off when nobody came around accusing him.

He developed the pictures and *really* saw what a naked woman looked like for the first time. He'd been so intent on taking the pictures before somebody came home and caught him that he hadn't stopped to savor his subject. He'd been in such a hurry that he hadn't even become sexually excited. But then Jerry Brudos' fantasies had never included *interaction* with a female; in his fantasies, women acted only on his bidding. He was the Master and they were only slaves.

His first impression of a nude female was that "she looked awful funny." But he soon took great pleasure in looking at his photographs while he handled his subject's stolen panties and bras, incorporating her, his prisoner, into his fantasy.

Later, his victim told police, "I knew who it was all the time; I wasn't fooled by that mask and his phony story about being locked in the barn, but I was afraid of him. I was scared if I told he would find out and he would kill me. . . ."

Eight months passed after the episode of forced picture-taking; Jerry wasn't worried about being discovered because nothing had come of it. But he had looked at those same pictures so often that they no longer produced the effect they once had. Besides that, they were smudged and tattered.

He needed a new captive.

Jerry Brudos couldn't find a girl who would date him. He was big and clumsy and suffered from teenage acne—"acne vulgaris," the doctors called it. His pimples were even more obvious when he blushed scarlet. When he was nervous, he ducked his head and his voice became a croak.

But it was more than his appearance and his awkwardness; there was something about Jerry Brudos that turned girls off, something scary that triggered an almost visceral reaction warning them to stay away from him.

Nevertheless, on a warm April evening in 1956, Jerry Brudos managed to lure a seventeen-year-old girl into his car on a ruse. He began to talk as if they were on a date together and she stared at him, baffled. She had only accepted a short ride.

Her bewilderment turned to panic when he stared straight ahead and drove faster, farther and farther away from the main roads. Finally, he pulled into an overgrown driveway and parked at a deserted farmhouse, its siding grayed from the weather, the wind blowing through its glassless windows.

She looked around and saw that they were miles from other houses, from anyone who might come to help her if she screamed.

Without a word, Jerry Brudos dragged the girl from his car and began to beat her. His fists rained down on her face and breasts, and she tasted her own blood warm and salty in her mouth. Fearing it would do no good, she screamed anyway as the huge, strange boy continued to pummel her. He pulled at her clothing, ordering her to strip for him. He wanted to see her naked, he said gasping. She twisted and kicked and tried to get away.

The sun would be setting soon, and she knew if she didn't get help, she would be dead by the time the sun rose again. She screamed with all her might, and his fist crunched sickeningly into her nose.

Fortunately, a couple from a farm down the road happened to be driving by just at that moment. The husband wrenched his steering wheel and turned quickly into the weed-choked yard. They saw the old car parked there, and the tall, heavy young man bent over someone on the ground beside it.

"She fell out of the car," he explained, reaching out to help the sobbing girl up. "She's just hysterical because it scared her."

The girl shook her head violently, trying to speak through her swollen mouth.

The couple looked on doubtfully, and the boy shrugged his shoulders. "Well, actually, what happened was that some weirdo attacked her. I came driving by and I stopped to help. She was fighting him off when I came up, and he took off through the fields over there."

This version didn't make any more impression on the couple than the first one, and they insisted on taking the girl—and Jerry Brudos, who went along quite meekly—back to their house, where they called the Oregon State Police.

Faced with the police, Jerry Brudos admitted that he had beaten the girl himself. He said he'd wanted to frighten her enough to make her take off her clothes so he could take pictures of her. He denied ever doing such a thing before. He seemed baffled by the incident himself; he felt his temper had just gotten the best of him. But police found his camera equipment in the trunk of his car, and recognized premeditation before the attack.

Jerry Brudos' victim was treated in a local Emergency Room and found to have extensive bruises and a badly broken nose.

Investigators searching Jerry's room on the farm in Dallas, Oregon, came upon his cache of women's clothing and shoes. And they found photographs. Pictures of women's undergarments and shoes, and photos of a nude girl. Jerry had an excuse for this, too. He insisted the pictures had been taken by another boy, and that he had only developed them.

"I had to . . .he said he'd beat me up if I didn't. . . ."

Jerry Brudos was arrested for assault and battery. He was referred to Polk County Juvenile Department which began a background investigation.

Eileen Brudos was outraged, and Henry was stunned. There had never been anyone on either side of the family who showed signs of mental illness or violence. *What in the world could be the matter with Jerry?*

A review of the case for which he was arrested, the presence of fetish items in his room, and a talk with the eighteen-year-old neighbor girl who now felt safe to come forward, convinced authorities that Jerry

Brudos had deeper problems than the average juvenile delinquent.

He was committed to Oregon State Hospital for evaluation and treatment in the spring of 1956.

Jerry Brudos seemed humbled and meek as he talked to a procession of psychiatrists. He said he was a sophomore in high school. He liked sports but he didn't like rough competition. "I don't like to fight or to push people around, or be pushed around—so I don't go out for any of the teams."

He gave his hobbies as working with radios, electronics, mechanics, and . . . photography. He had belonged to 4–H, Boy Scouts, the Farmer's Union.

The Jerry Brudos who sat in Oregon State Hospital seemed impossibly remote from a sadistic sex criminal. He blushed crimson when asked about his sex life—or rather his lack of sexual experience. He said he "suffered" from nocturnal emissions—"wet dreams"—about every two months. He tried to lead a clean life; he didn't drink. He didn't smoke.

No, he had never had a sexual relationship with a girl. He had never even been out alone with a girl; sometimes, he had been in large groups where girls were present. Yes, he had taken the pictures of the neighbor girl and she had been the first naked woman he had ever seen.

Doctors were a little puzzled, searching for a diagnosis. One psychiatrist wrote on April 16, 1956:

"The boy does not appear to be grossly mentally ill. He comes shyly into the interview situation and sits down in dejected fashion to talk with great embarrassment about his difficulty. It is difficult for him to form any relationship with the examining physician although he does warm up slightly through the course of the interview. He is precisely oriented in all spheres; speech rate, thought rate, and psychomotor activities are within normal limits. Flow of thinking is relevant, logical, and coherent. He tends to be evasive on a basis of his acute embarrassment and is somewhat rambling and verbose in trying to tell his story. He appears to be somewhat depressed at the present time and his predominant mood would appear to be of depressed, dejected embarrassment. His affect is appropriate to thought content. *There is no evidence of suicide, homicide, or destructive urges.* He feels that he sometimes has trouble controlling his temper but that it has never got him into trouble except on this last occasion when he maintains that he cannot remember too clearly exactly what he did but was told that the girl received a broken nose. There is no evidence of hallucinations, delusions, or illusions. He denies any sense of fear except over what is going to happen to him, and he says he has some sense of guilt over having got into trouble but does not feel particularly guilty over having taken the photographs. . . . Intellectually, he is functioning well within the limits of his educational background. His insight and judgment are questionable; he feels that there must be something the matter with him and he hopes that he will be able to find out and have it cured here. . . .

The provisional diagnosis of Jerry Brudos' problem was: "Adjustment reaction of adolescence with sexual deviation, fetishism."

Jerry was not a full-time patient at the mental hospital. During the day, he was allowed to attend high school at North Salem High School. He moved among the other students as a nonentity, a tall, pudgy youth with raging acne.

He was smart, probably brilliant, in mathematics and science, and yet no one remembers him. None of his teachers. None of his fellow students. Years later, one of his defense attorneys would realize with a start that he and Jerry had been in the same homeroom at North Salem High. But the lawyer could remember no more about Jerry Brudos in high school than anyone else could.

When he became infamous, teachers and peers *tried* to remember Jerry. They still couldn't. He had moved through North Salem High and left no ripple behind.

He was a loner. The odd duck, hurrying through the halls with his head bent. His after-school residence at the state hospital was kept secret. All anyone at North Salem High knew was that he never came to the football and basketball games and never showed up at the dances, where Elvis Presley's records of "Blue Suede Shoes" and "Heartbreak Hotel" played over and over.

He belonged to another world.

Jerry Brudos' fantasies, as black and horrific as they were, remained his own. When he stared at the pretty high school girls, at their clothing, and especially at their wonderful shoes, he did it covertly.

At the mental hospital, Jerry talked often with the doctors. A second diagnosis was "borderline schizophrenic reaction" a handy catch-all diagnosis of the era.

Jerry remained at the hospital for eight or nine months. Henry and Eileen Brudos were adamant that they didn't want him home until he was cured of whatever ailed him.

But before a year had passed, he *did* come home to the family farm in Dallas. Jerry had not been missed much. Eileen had been working at a wool mill, and Henry worked the farm and had a job in town. Larry was doing well in college. Jerry was the only problem they had.

In the end, the staff at Oregon State Hospital had determined that Jerry Brudos was not that far removed from normal. A bit immature, certainly, overly shy, and given to tall stories, but not particularly dangerous. When he left the hospital, he was advised to "grow up."

Back in Corvallis, Jerry returned to high school. There was 202 students in his graduating class. He enrolled in audiovisual and stagecraft courses for his electives. It is somewhat ironic that this noncommunicative youth should pick courses that dealt principally *with* communication, with reaching out and touching others through the radio or from the stage. What he could not seem to do in a face-to-face encounter, he apparently sought to do through the media. His goal was to obtain an FCC license so that he could be employed at a radio or television station.

He was quite adept at electronics; he has been described by some who knew him as "brilliant" in that field, and, in the same breath, "lazy." He was skilled at electrical wiring, too, and he was a fair backyard mechanic.

Jerry Brudos graduated 142nd in the class of 202, with a grade-point average of 2.1, just above a C. He attended Oregon State University for a short time, Salem Technical Vocational School for a while, and dabbled at a few other advanced schools.

On March 9, 1959, Jerry joined the U.S. Army and was sent to Fort Ord, California, and subsequently to Fort Gordon, Georgia, for basic and advanced training in the Signal Corps. He eventually achieved the rank of E-2. With his skill and interest in communication and electronics, the Army might have been the perfect choice for him.

But his obsessions had never left him.

He became convinced that a Korean girl had come into the barracks one night and crawled into his bunk and tried to seduce him. "I didn't want her and I came up fighting and beat her badly."

The dream woman returned on several occasions, and Jerry wondered that none of his barracks mates teased him about it. At length he decided that there was no real woman—that she was only a dream. No one complained of the noise that accompanied his beating of the woman. No one even noticed when she came in the night to tease and fondle him.

Jerry worried that he hated the woman so much he wanted to beat her and kill her. He went to the Army chaplain, who referred him to Captain Theodore J. Barry, the staff psychiatrist. Dr. Barry determined that Jerry was not fit for the service because of his bizarre obsessions and recommended discharge for him under AR 635-208. On October 15, 1959, Jerry was discharged—disappointed and wondering why the Army should let him go for such a minor thing.

Jerry Brudos, twenty years old now, returned to Corvallis, Oregon, after his discharge and moved into the two-bedroom house where his parents lived. He was allowed to live in the second bedroom; but then

Larry came home from college. As always, Larry came first. He was given the extra bedroom, and Jerry was relegated to a shed on the property. He covered the windows so no one could peer in at him and "because I wanted to keep out the light."

His old anger at his mother surged back. Larry had the good room; he had the shed.

Both Mr. Brudos and Larry came to Jerry and advised him to give up trying to find favor in his mother's eyes. "She will never treat you well. She never has and she never will." They seemed sympathetic to him—but as impotent as he was in trying to change things.

He stayed away from home as much as possible, and when he was on the Brudos property he sequestered himself in his darkened shack and tried to shut out the knowledge that his mother still seemed to be in control of his life.

One evening, Jerry went over to Salem on an errand. He spotted a pretty young woman walking near the telephone office. She wore a bright red outfit, and he could not take his eyes off her. He followed her, excited by the scarlet clothing. She did not realize he was just behind her as she turned into the doorway of an apartment house. Only when she was in the dim, deserted foyer did she hear the soft footfall right behind her. She turned, frightened. She opened her mouth to speak, but before she could utter a sound, Jerry simply closed his hands around her neck and choked her until she fell to the floor, semiconscious. Jerry looked down at her, lying helpless there, and debated what he should do to her.

She was lucky: he only stole her shoes.

It happened again in Portland. The stalking of a woman who wore sexy shoes. Again, he choked his quarry, but this time the woman fought back and he managed to make off with only one shoe.

Back in his shack, he slept with the shoes, remembering the power he'd had over their owners—if only for a short time. Somehow, this made him feel stronger now when he had to deal with his mother.

— 2 —

Despite his disfavor at home, Jerry Brudos was functioning effectively in his chosen career goal. He obtained his FCC license and, with it, a job as an operating engineer at a Corvallis radio station. It gave him a modicum of self-esteem, and he seemed, at least outwardly, to be less of a loner. He had a skilled job—something that few men could qualify for. He bull-shitted with the station employees, and they accepted him.

He was a big man. At six feet and 180 pounds, he had far outstripped his father's five feet, four inches.

He was still a virgin.

Jerry Brudos had an old car that he had fixed up, and he was eager to have a steady girl of his own. Although he distrusted women generally, he thought he might find a woman who would be perfect—someone who would be totally committed to him—and someone who would welcome him sexually whenever he wanted. Once he found her, he would keep her away from the rest of the world. She would belong to him alone.

Jerry met his woman when he was almost twenty-three, met her through an unusual channel. Since he was not adept socially, he found it hard to meet women. There was a young boy who came into the station to watch Jerry work at his control panel, a kid who "bugged" Jerry with questions and with his constant visits.

But the kid brought Darcie to him. One day Jerry asked the boy if he knew any girls that Jerry could date, and the boy, eager to please, introduced him to Darcie Metzler.

Darcie would pay dearly in years to come for the

romance that began as if it had come right out of a popular love song.

Darcie was seventeen, a pretty, big-eyed young woman with thick dark hair, when she met Jerry Brudos. She was very quiet and shy, but not unpopular with boys. She dated frequently and went out with boys she describes as "good-looking." She had grown up in a family that was strictly dominated by her father, a man of Germanic extraction, and she was chafing to get out and be on her own. She was too submissive to rebel—she had never been the type to question authority, and she loved her parents. But she dreamed of having her own home, where she could make her own decisions.

She was exactly the type of woman Jerry had been looking for.

When the little boy brought Jerry to her house and introduced him for the first time, she wasn't very impressed. In fact, she didn't like him at all. His clothes were neither neat nor stylish. Her first view of him was of an average-looking man in rumpled, paint-spattered pants. She thought he could have dressed up a little when he was meeting her for the first time. He had thinning blond-red hair and a bit of a double chin; he certainly wasn't as attractive as the guys she usually dated.

"I probably wouldn't have accepted a date with him at all—except that he asked me to go swimming, and I love to swim."

For some reason—perhaps because she was so shy herself—Darcie didn't threaten Jerry or make him feel angry. She laughed at his jokes and made him feel good.

"He was full of fun and full of jokes," she recalls. "I was so shy that I couldn't even get up in school to recite or answer questions, and he seemed so confident."

It is quite possible that Jerry Brudos could not have impressed a woman of his own age so much, but Darcie Metzler was six years younger than he. She was impressed with his job and with him. She gave him the attention and admiration he'd never found before.

He was very tender with her, demonstrating niceties of courtship that the teenage boys she knew didn't understand. He pulled out her chair for her, opened doors, bought small gifts and flowers. He put her "on a pedestal," and she liked that.

And to ensure that she would be absolutely dazzled by Jerry, there was the fact that her parents didn't like him and said so. Nothing drives a girl quicker into a lover's arms than parental disapproval.

Brudos didn't like his mother-in-law-to-be much better than he liked his own mother—which was not at all. He found her "stubborn and independent—like me." He didn't like Darcie's father, either. "He felt because he was older that he could decide what we would do, where we would go—all of that."

Jerry was very jealous of Darcie. Fiercely jealous. She was flattered by that in the beginning, considering jealousy to be part of true love. Since she was spending all of her time with Jerry anyway and had no interest in any other man, she felt protected by his possessiveness.

In retrospect, after all the horror had been acted out and had almost destroyed her, Darcie believes that she never really loved Jerry Brudos. In 1962, she thought she did. "While my home life was a good one, there was this feeling that 'getting married' would be much better than listening to your parents."

Brudos recalled their betrothal more pragmatically. "I wanted someone to sleep with, and she wanted out of her home."

He had never had intercourse with a woman when he met Darcie, despite all of his erotic fantasies. That lack was remedied soon after they began dating. Apparently Darcie found him normal sexually—or perhaps she had nothing to compare his performance to. She did not know about his background of mental illness.

She certainly did not know of his fetishism or of his rage toward women.

Because her parents were so adamantly opposed to Jerry, the two lovers decided that if she were to become pregnant, they would be allowed to marry. Darcie proved to be instantly fertile, and they were married within six weeks.

Darcie was thrilled with the event. She did not consider that theirs had been a "shotgun" wedding, because she had planned the pregnancy and because she felt she had a sensitive, successful husband.

Jerry was relieved. He had been terrified that Darcie would meet his brother and would leave him in favor of Larry. Since Larry had usurped all good things from him so far, he was sure that he would take Darcie away too.

A daughter, Megan, was born to the couple in 1962, and the marriage seemed to be a happy one for the first three years. Jerry found jobs easily enough, although he couldn't seem to hold on to them. It was no great concern to Darcie because he could always find another. He spent a great deal of money on presents for her on holidays and anniversaries, and he continued to be kind and considerate. She was so busy with the baby that she didn't tumble to the fact that she was virtually a prisoner in her own home.

She didn't know that when she said or did something that made her husband "depressed," he prowled and stole underwear and shoes to make him feel better. She had not seen the flashes of temper that "scared the hell out of" people who knew him.

Jerry's choice for their intimate behavior was her guideline too. When they were home together, they were nude. They continued to "run around the house without clothes" until Megan grew from an infant to a toddler and Darcie balked at being naked in front of the child.

And Jerry, always an avid—if sometimes secret—photographer, insisted on taking nude pictures of Darcie. He had taken a few shots before their marriage, and more on their wedding night. She didn't feel comfortable with it, but he assured her that she was his wife and it was all right. She didn't mind the black-and-white snaps because he could develop them in his own darkroom, but she objected to color slides. They had to be processed commercially. Jerry had an answer for that, too. He explained that if he took the first and the last slides in a series of pleasant scenery or something else innocuous, nobody would ever look at them. Big labs process too much film to look at every single picture.

"Darcie," he explained, "they look at the first or the last—and that's all."

She relented, but she never felt good about it.

Jerry's suggested poses were so strange. He directed the naked Darcie to ride on Megan's tricycle, toward him, away from him. Darcie's buttocks bulged over the tiny seat, her breasts were draped over the handlebars. When she saw the finished print, she winced. She begged him to rip the pictures up, and he promised he would.

But he didn't.

Some of her husband's requests were bizarre. Jerry had Darcie pose, sitting on the floor, with a nylon pulled over her face so that her features were distorted into a grotesque mask. And, as always, she was nude. Some of the pictures featured Darcie wearing nothing but spike-heeled black patent-leather shoes.

One day, those pictures, along with so many others, would become police exhibits. Darcie Brudos, who had been embarrassed that someone in an anonymous photo lab might see her naked image, could never have imagined that her nakedness would be seen by scores of strangers, that she would be questioned in court about why she would pose for such kinky pictures.

Nor could she have possibly foreseen why her private sex-life with Jerry would be such a subject of speculation.

Even when they weren't taking pictures, Jerry wanted Darcie to wear high heels all the time—not just when they went out, but when she did housework. They made her back hurt, and aggravated her bad knee. She tried to explain that to Jerry, but her arguments seemed to depress him.

In a way—a way she could not possibly know at the time—Darcie Metzler Brudos had become the fantasy girl that the sixteen-year-old Jerry Brudos had wanted to place in a secret tunnel, someone his own to do with what he wanted.

She usually went along with him. She was not an assertive woman. Her father had been dominant; now her husband was dominant. She was a little afraid of him, yet could not say why. She compromised again and again with her hulking husband in a marriage that she has described as "very good" at first, and then, as three or four years passed, "stranger and stranger." The shy, soft little woman wanted only a happy home—but achieving that became increasingly difficult.

Darcie was hurt to see that Jerry was so removed and disinterested in their daughter. "He was very distant with Megan." If the toddler tried to crawl in Brudos' lap or to kiss him, he invariably pushed her away. He avoided any physical contact with his own child, and Megan sensed that she somehow displeased her father. On one atypical occasion, Brudos took Megan on an outing to feed ducks, and the child was overjoyed at receiving attention from him, but it was only an isolated incident and Brudos returned behind the invisible wall he'd built between himself and Megan.

Darcie wondered if he resented Megan because she took so much of her own time. That may have been a partial explanation for Brudos' behavior. It may have been that he did not trust himself with the girl-child, that he felt an incestuous attraction. If the latter was true, Megan was saved from something far worse than neglect.

In Brudos' eyes, Darcie was perfect. He had such a tenuous lid on his underlying violence, but if she had managed to remain completely docile, submissive, and obedient, he might have maintained the status quo longer than he did.

She could not. Such small things depressed Jerry. Small mistakes grew into gargantuan betrayals in his mind.

The Brudoses moved from one rented home to another—twenty houses or more in their seven years together. From Corvallis to Portland, and back again, and then for a while to Salem. Darcie got used to packing everything and moving on, but she always dreaded the news that they would have to move again. She knew Jerry was smart and clever with anything electrical, and she wondered why he couldn't hold a job. She wanted to have her own home, someplace permanent where she could put up curtains and plant bulbs and know she would be around to see them come up. But she never was; they were always living someplace else when spring came. And she began to worry for Megan, who would be starting school soon. What would it do to the child to have to adjust continually to new schools?

Jerry had done the same thing already, of course— moving constantly up and down the West Coast when he was a child. If he had done it, he didn't see why Megan couldn't.

In 1965 Jerry had a job at an electronics firm in West Salem, working as a technician. His employer found him a "Casper Milquetoast kind of guy." But he also recalls him as "the most brilliant electronically oriented mind I've ever seen. There wasn't anything he didn't know about electricity and circuitry."

The boss liked him well enough, although he seemed a sissy and totally nonaggressive. Brudos worked in the company for months, went fishing with the boss, and never, never showed any signs of temper. He was placid and amenable to suggestion. He just didn't apply himself, and that was the only explanation his employer could give for his being stuck in a technician's job. "With his First Class FCC license, he could have run any television or radio station in the country. But his only ambition was to read—read and study— and that was the end for him. He always carried a bound portfolio with him, filled with letters of recommendation. Each letter was encased in plastic, and he was really proud of those things. They were from college professors and electronics experts—character references. He must have shown them to me four or five times; he wanted people to think he was important."

One thing Jerry Brudos never discussed with the

men at the plant. That was women. He presented himself as a solid family man, and he never participated in the sometimes ribald conversations of his fellow workers. He didn't drink, and he didn't smoke, and his employer was sorry to lose him when he left.

He came back to visit after a year or so. He still wasn't running a television or radio station, not even a small one.

Brudos had an explanation for that, a story that was a total fabrication. He said he'd enlisted in the Navy and had been injured in the explosion of a shell aboard ship. He recalled that the accident had killed two of his buddies, and that he had spent a year in a naval hospital himself, his injuries so severe that he had become eligible for a service pension. It was a patent lie—all of it. Since he had been released from the Army for psychiatric reasons, the Navy would never have accepted him. His former boss didn't know that, of course, but the story sounded fishy.

And yet even with Brudos' transparent attempt to make himself a hero, his ex-employer couldn't help liking the guy. He was pitiable, sitting there with his usual hangdog expression, his shoulders sloped forward as if he expected rejection. So, what the hell— he'd tried to make himself sound macho with some fairy tale. His old boss took Jerry home to meet the family, and didn't question him about what he'd *really* been up to while he was gone.

Two events occurred in Jerry Brudos' life in 1967 that seemed to unleash the perverted obsessions that had lain smoldering inside him for so long. Given the extent of his aberration, some thing at some time would have triggered him. The monster within was growing restless. His migraines were accelerating both in number and in magnitude and he was experiencing what he called "blackouts."

He had managed to alleviate his depressions—the terrible black, hopeless feelings that swept over him when he thought Darcie did not love him enough— with his nocturnal prowls to steal underwear and shoes. Each time, for a while, his stolen garments made him feel better. But his spells of feeling good lasted such a short time.

When Darcie became pregnant again, Jerry was enthusiastic—far more than he had been over her pregnancy with Megan. It was almost as if he was going through the gestation right along with her. He wanted to do it all; he wanted to be right there in the delivery room when his son was born. He had no doubt at all that it would be a son.

His own father had not been very easy to reach, closed up, really, when he'd needed to talk, or just plain not there. But, given the choice between his parents, he thought his father at least had tried the best he could. Jerry, though, would be a good father to his son—right from the beginning.

In a way, and on an unconscious level, Jerry foresaw his son's birth as a rebirth for himself too. When he saw that baby emerge into the world, he would be released from the bad things he had been doing.

He thought Darcie understood how important it was that he should be in the delivery room with her. He believed he could trust her to send for him when it was time.

She didn't. He tried to follow her into the delivery room, and found his way blocked. The doctor had left firm orders that he was not to be allowed in! Even the announcement that he had a son didn't mitigate his anguish, and he could hardly bear to look at the infant at first.

He was plunged into despair when Darcie came home and told him that *she* had asked the doctor to keep him out.

"*Why?*" he asked her, bewildered. "You told me I could be there."

"I didn't want you to watch another man play with me," she said. "I didn't think it was right."

It was such an odd way to describe a physician's part in the birth of a baby. But, considering how he had always told Darcie he could not bear to have "another man touch you," she may have thought that *any* touching would disturb her husband.

Tears sprang to Jerry's eyes, and he could not be

consoled. Instead, he went out into the night and stole another pair of shoes. This time, it wasn't enough. He was still full of rage and hurt.

A short while later, he was in downtown Portland and saw a girl wearing a pretty pair of shoes. Rather than knocking her down and stealing her shoes, he decided that he would follow her until she went home and take the shoes from her there. He watched her for hours, staying just behind her while she shopped for groceries, following her onto the bus and jumping out the doors behind her just as they began to close. He watched her go into an apartment building, followed, and noted which window was hers.

He waited until he was sure she was asleep, and then he crept into her apartment. It was exciting to have varied his procedure this way, to know what the woman looked like who slept so close to where he fumbled in her closet. He told himself that he didn't want her; he had only come for her shoes.

But she woke up and saw the dark shadowy figure kneeling on her bedroom floor. Before she could cry out, he was beside her on the bed. He had to choke her then because she might be able to tell someone what he looked like. He would make her unconscious before she could turn on the lamp beside her bed. Her throat was so soft, and he applied just enough pressure with his big hands. She sighed and went limp.

He had not thought of raping her, but having her so helpless stimulated him. He moved his hands over her body. For that moment, she belonged to him, and he felt a powerful erection, the strongest he had ever had.

He raped her there in the dark, and when he was finished with her, he took the shoes and left.

They were the best shoes he'd ever stolen.

The birth of his son—without him—had been the worst thing that had ever happened to him. He had erased the disappointment of being robbed of that experience by having the woman.

The second event of 1967 almost killed Jerry. He had made his living as an electrician since he'd left the radio station in Corvallis. He was very cautious, and certainly knowledgeable about safety precautions, yet he came very close to electrocuting himself.

He was working at one bench and reached across to connect a live wire in his hand to terminals on another bench. Instantly his body became rigid as a jolt of power ran through him, 480 volts raced from his right arm through his chest and down his left arm, and the force of it picked him up and threw him across his bench and onto the floor.

He was not rendered unconscious, but he was dazed and burned. And his neck was injured, cervical damage resulting that would stay with him.

A weaker man would have been killed, but Brudos survived. Indeed, he was never even hospitalized.

And so he was quite well and strong enough to lift heavy objects—even the deadweight of a body or an automobile engine—by January 26, 1968. He had beaten women, and stolen their lingerie and shoes, and choked them, and, finally, raped one. But he had never killed a woman.

Not until Linda Slawson came to his door hoping to sell him a set of encyclopedias. . . .

—— 3 ——

Ironically, even as her husband's mental problems had progressed into homicidal rage, Darcie Brudos thought that maybe their marriage was getting better. He had been so unhappy about the events surrounding Jason's birth, but he seemed to have forgiven her once she had explained her motivations to him. He became enthralled with Jason, showing the youngster so much more attention than he'd ever shown their first child. He took Jason with him when he went on errands, and he talked about teaching Jason how to use the tools in his workshop—when he grew up a little. It hurt Darcie that he still ignored Megan, but it was nice that he seemed to accept Jason.

He let Darcie herself have a little more freedom, allowing her to visit girlfriends or to bowl. She knew he wasn't crazy about having his mother baby-sit for Megan while she was away, but he didn't really put his foot down. He was always downstairs in his workshop anyway, fiddling with some electrical project or other, or out with his friends buying engine parts in junkyards.

His headaches, however, had grown worse. She had to keep the children quiet so much of the time because any sound seemed to cause him excruciating pain when he had one of his migraines. It was easier just to take them both with her and go spend the days with girlfriends where the kids could be themselves. She thought maybe the electrical accident had caused the headache problems to be so bad now. But she couldn't persuade Jerry to go to a doctor about it.

The brief spate of calm after Jason's birth didn't last very long. Darcie blamed herself for part of the trouble. She no longer enjoyed sex with her husband. She

wasn't even sure why, but when he accused her of
being uninterested in him, or disgusted by his touch,
she had to agree with him—even though she would
not admit it out loud. They weren't kids on a honey-
moon any longer; she couldn't go dashing around the
house naked now. She *hated* posing for nude photos,
obeying his instructions to pose this way and that.

He wanted her to dress up "fancy" all the time,
saying that other women looked good and she didn't.
But you couldn't wear sexy clothes while you were
doing dishes and washing diapers.

He wanted to go out dancing. Well, that hurt her
bad knee, and wearing spike heels all the time made
her back hurt. When she told him so, he looked offended and drove off somewhere. She had no idea
where he went or what he did.

She knew he was very sensitive, and she sensed that
she should not argue with him or disobey him, but she
was no longer the pliable girl she had been when they
were married. She wanted something beyond the cloistered life in which only the two of them existed.

Jerry lost his job in Portland and in the spring of
1968 they decided to leave the house at Forty-seventh
and Hawthorne and move to Salem. In a way, Darcie
was glad to go—especially when they found the nice
little house on Center Street. It was not a lavish house,
but it was kind of cute and cozy. Gray shake and close
to the ground. It had a big yard full of evergreens,
roses, and flowering trees. There was a fence around
the yard, just white chicken wire, but sturdy enough to
prevent the children from running out into Center
Street, a main thoroughfare in Salem. There was an
attic for storage, and the garage had a workshop portion where Jerry could set up all the gear he'd accumulated. The garage wasn't hooked onto the house itself,
but connected by a breezeway. Jerry looked at the
place and deemed it perfect for them.

Darcie had friends in Salem, and she liked living in
a smaller city than Portland.

For Jerry Brudos, coming back to Salem was the
completion of a circle. The Oregon State Mental Hospital where he had been incarcerated a dozen years

earlier after beating his teenage date was only a few blocks down Center Street from the gray house. Its proximity didn't seem to bother him; he never spoke of it at all.

Salem, Oregon, is one of the lovelier cities on the West Coast, and the capitol city of Oregon. The Capitol Building itself is gleaming white and topped with an immense statue of a pioneer, a golden figure that can be seen for miles. The parking strips of Salem are planted with roses that bloom from May through December. There are carefully preserved mansions alongside modern homes, and the land outside Salem is verdant and productive. Green beans, corn, peas, hops, and strawberries grow abundantly in the Willamette Valley, and Salem has processing plants where the crops are canned and frozen.

There are paper mills in Salem too, and when the wind is right, their acrid smell laces the air, assaults the nose, and leaves a metallic taste on the tongue.

The brightest high-school students in Oregon are drawn to Willamette University in Salem, and the politicians come to the legislature. Others, as Jerry Brudos once had been, are locked up in the state's institutions—all located in Marion County (except for the boys' reformatory in Woodburn, a few miles north). The Oregon State Prison, the Hillcrest School for Girls, the Oregon State Mental Hospital, and the Fairview School for the Developmentally Disabled surround Salem. Some of the inmates escape, but most are only paroled or furloughed or dismissed from custody. Many of them remain in the Salem area to live in halfway houses or blend, however roughly, into the mainstream.

Salem police and Marion County sheriff's personnel expect a little more trouble than most lawmen—the percentage of the population that is a little strange exceeds that of most areas.

Jerry Brudos did not stand out as "strange"; he was too covert for that, and he seldom left the little house on Center Street. Despite the job opportunities offered through the food and paper-mill industries, he was not able to find work. Maybe he didn't look that hard; his headaches were bad, and his neck hurt.

And he had so much on his mind.

He moped around the house or puttered in his shop out in the garage, and Jerry packed on pounds. There were new rolls of fat around his waist and under his chin. One day, Darcie mentioned to him that he seemed to be gaining weight, and he grunted and disappeared into another room in the house. He was gone for a short time. When he returned, his wife was shocked to see Jerry standing before her, dressed in a woman's bra—stuffed with something to look like breasts—a girdle, stockings with garters, and the biggest pair of black pointy-toed high-heeled shoes she'd ever seen. Somehow, he'd managed to tuck his genitals inside the girdle so that he almost looked like a woman, turning and posing for her. All he needed was a wig. . . .

Jerry looked so peculiar, a great big freckled man standing there in women's underwear—funny, really . . . but not funny. Darcie laughed nervously, but she was frightened and embarrassed. It seemed a little sick.

Darcie was naive. She didn't know what a fetish was. She didn't know about transvestites or sexual psychopaths. She knew that some men were gay, but Jerry had always been entirely masculine. Their own sex life had always been straight when it came to intercourse. He'd never asked her to do anything that was kinky or repulsive. Nothing beyond posing for nude pictures.

He seemed a little disappointed at her reaction. There was an awkward silence, and then he left the room. When he came back, he looked like himself again.

She wondered where he'd gotten the girdle and bra, but she didn't ask him. She didn't want to make him angry or upset. Because it made her worry when she thought about her husband dressing up like a girl, she put it out of her mind. She had enough to worry about: money for bills, and keeping the children quiet, and trying not to irritate Jerry.

She could not have known, could never have visualized in her worst nightmares, just how bad things were going to get.

4

As the Brudoses settled into their Center Street home in Salem in the summer of 1968, a detective worked in his offices in Salem's hundred-year-old city hall, perhaps a dozen blocks northwest of them. Though he was a twenty-year police veteran, and though fifteen years of that time had been spent in the detective unit, where he'd seen his share of violent crimes, Jim Stovall could not foresee how bad things would get either. And when it was over, he would deem the Brudos case the most shocking of his long career.

Every heinous criminal has his nemesis, his alter ego—the one detective out of dozens whose whole existence is taken up for a time with catching his quarry. Jerry Brudos—for all of his macabre fantasies—was a most intelligent man, a planner and a schemer. He would not be caught easily, and, once caught, he would be difficult to break.

If there is a working detective in America who could be the model for the brilliant investigators portrayed in fiction, it would be Jim Stovall. That he happened to be living and working in Salem, Oregon, in the black period of killings in 1968 and 1969 was one of the few bright spots in a terrible story.

In the summer of 1968, Brudos and Stovall did not know each other, although it is very possible that they passed each other on the streets of Salem, that Brudos drove past the looming old city hall, that Stovall drove past the gray house on Center Street. And, oddly but not mystically, long before he ever confronted Jerry Brudos, Stovall would draw up a psychological profile of the killer he sought that was as clear and detailed as if he were psychic.

But that was later, much later than the sunny, rose-filled days of mid-1968—because, at that time, Brudos had not yet begun to carry out the rest of his killing plans. He still waited, basking in the afterglow of the perfection of Linda Slawson's murder.

Jim Stovall and Jerry Brudos had a few things in common. They each had a wife and a son and a daughter. Both of them had been in the armed services at one time. And both of them were planners and given to attention to detail. That was all. One of them worked to save lives. The other . . .

Some good cops are cerebral and some work with gut feelings—the "seat-of-the-pants" cop who knows what he knows but cannot tell you why. Stovall is that rare cop who is both, and woe to the criminal who wanders into his line of vision.

Jim Stovall is a tall, handsome man with clear gray eyes, waving iron-gray hair, and the physique of the athlete he is. He looks like a bank president, or a TV newsman, or—yes—the glorified image of a slick detective. He looks a great deal like the actor Rory Calhoun, but would be embarrassed if someone should mention it to him.

In the Second World War, Stovall served in both the U.S. Army and the U.S. Marine Corps, where he was a rifle-range coach. When the armistice was declared, it seemed a natural progression that he should sign up with the Salem Police Department.

Like most veteran cops, Stovall has lived through hairy incidents. As a rookie with less than a year on the force, he responded to the most dangerous radio squawk an officer can get: "Family fight." An enraged husband had left the family home after threatening to come back and kill his wife. Since a fair percentage of angry husbands do just that, there was a "want" on the suspect's vehicle. Stovall spotted the car, signaled it to move over to the side of the road, and approached the driver's door from the rear, stopping just behind the driver. Instead of the driver's license he'd requested, the man came up with a Luger—pointed at Stovall's heart.

Stovall could see that the man was wild-eyed and

shaky, likely to shoot. He kept his voice and his eyes steady as he spoke. "Look . . . you don't know me too well—so I'll give you a chance to point that in another direction. . . ."

The driver's finger tightened on the trigger, and Stovall could almost hear his mind deciding what to do. They stared at each other for five . . . ten . . . fifteen seconds, and then the gunman laid his weapon down on the seat beside him and surrendered.

Had things gone badly, the Salem Police Department would have lost one hell of a cop.

Stovall was the top marksman in the department for eighteen years, and still shoots an occasional 98 or 99 on the FBI's PPC course. One night, he was staked out in the hallway of a building where a rash of burglaries had occurred. After a boring night, he heard the tinkle of broken glass somewhere in the building. The would-be burglar met Stovall in the hall, where the officer flashed his light into the man's face and challenged him. The suspect broke and ran into a room, locking the door behind him. Stovall aimed at the shadow behind the glass door and fired his .38. He then heard a crash, followed by the sound of running feet.

Stovall thought he had missed the man, until a doctor in a Salem hospital's emergency room reported that a man had come in for treatment of a "nail wound." Stovall went to the hospital and recognized the man he'd seen for a split second in the rays of his flashlight. The burglaries stopped, and the thief recovered at leisure in prison.

Promoted into the detective unit after only five years on the force, Stovall availed himself of all training opportunities. He has a certificate in legal medicine from the Harvard University Medical School, has had many hours of study at Willamette University's Law School, and studied police business administration at the International City Managers' Association Institute of Training in Chicago. He has attended the Southern Police Institute in Louisville, Kentucky, and schools on visual-investigation analysis and link-analysis-charting techniques given by the California Department of Justice. He has also studied advanced psychology and hypnosis. And he is an expert photographer and a licensed pilot.

A dog-eared square of paper is always tacked where Stovall can see it above his desk: "THE ELEMENTS OF SCIENTIFIC PROOF MUST BE PRESENT TO ESTABLISH AND SUBSTANTIATE A SCIENTIFIC CONCLUSION."

And Jim Stovall has solved some homicide cases that defied solution, by meticulous attention to detail, by seeking and eventually finding that minuscule bit of physical evidence that starts the first ravel in a case that seems impenetrable.

When a lovely twenty-three-year-old woman was beaten and stabbed to death in her bedroom in Salem, Stovall determined that the bludgeon weapon was a broken soft-drink bottle, its green fragments glittering in the sheets that covered her.

Every man the girl had ever known or dated was located and questioned, amd all of them were cleared. Then the victim's mother remembered a seventeen-year-old boy she had encountered on the street. "He said he'd been away for a year, and he mentioned to me that he would like to call my daughter and come over to see her sometime—but I don't think he ever called or came around, because she never mentioned him."

Jim Stovall recognized the youth's name—he'd been arrested for minor juvenile offenses and there was a warrant out for him on a burglary charge. When he was taken into custody, he grudgingly let the detective have his clothing and shoes for lab examination.

There were a few specks of dark red on the suspect's clothes—too little to classify as to type. But in the heel of the youth's shoes, Stovall saw a tiny sliver of green glass.

At the Oregon State Crime Lab the shard of glass was compared with the bottle fragments found at the death scene under a scanning electron microscope and then in an electrospectrometer with a laser attachment for elements and light refraction. *The samples were identical.* They could only have come from the same batch of bottles, a circumstance that indicated it was highly probable that they had come from the *same* bottle.

Faced with that information, the killer confessed that he had killed the victim when she refused his sexual advances.

One of the strangest cases Jim Stovall ever solved was a classic "man found shot dead in a locked room with no weapon in sight."

Investigating a report on a man who had disappeared from his usual haunts, Stovall and his partner, Sergeant John Kelly, checked the doors of the man's home and found them all locked. The front door was open, but a locked screen door prevented entry. The windows were all locked from the inside. Stovall broke the screen-door lock and stepped inside. The occupant lay facedown several feet from the front door. His right hand still clutched a nutcracker, and his mouth was full of nut meats. Until the dead man was turned over, it looked as if he had succumbed to a heart attack. But, faceup, there was a small red hole in the front of his shirt, over his heart.

Stovall and Kelly looked for the gun that had to be there. An odd suicide, but then, suicides are not normal under any circumstances. Since all the doors and windows had been locked from the inside, and since the dead man was alone in the house, the only answer had to be suicide—unless one believed that a killer had arrived and left via the chimney like Santa Claus. But there was no gun anywhere on the premises, so how could a suicide be explained?

Neighbors were quick to offer a motive for murder. The dead man had been seeing another man's wife, and the other man was insanely jealous. It was not at all surprising that the victim was dead. What was curious was *how*.

Stovall, who takes as many as one hundred photographs at homicide scenes, shuffled through his developed pictures and stopped when he came to a shot of the screen door. He enlarged it, and enlarged it again, and again.

And there it was. A slight gap in the screen. The bullet had been a .25-caliber, quite small. When it passed through the wire mesh of the screen, it had made a hole, all right—and then the metal strands had snapped back almost as good as new. Unable to be seen by the naked eye, the piercing of the screen showed up in the photo lab. Stovall had weighed the variables, and figured that was the only way. Even if he couldn't see it, he expected to find a tear there.

Jim Stovall's main goal is to find the truth—not to put people behind bars. If the truth sets a "good" suspect free, those are the breaks; it only means that the answer has not yet been ferreted out.

One Salem husband came very close to going to jail for the murder of his wife because a pathologist skimped on the autopsy.

"Failure to perform a complete autopsy or to save material for toxicological analysis is a dangerous practice—even if you have a suitable answer at the time," Stovall says.

In murder, of all human phenomena, things *are* seldom what they seem. In the mysterious death of the forty-year-old victim, it looked clearly as if her architect husband had killed her because he was tired of dealing with her emotional problems. Men have shuffled their wives off for far less.

Stovall and his crew found the woman dead one summer afternoon, lying in her kitchen in a welter of blood with a wound on the top of her head. The medical examiner ruled it a homicide—probably by beating and strangling. Her throat had the hemorrhages peculiar to strangulation, and the state of rigor was well advanced when she was found. Time of death was pegged at ten A.M. because of the rigor mortis.

"There was something not quite right," Stovall recalls. "Her hands were flexed in such a way that I was suspicious."

The husband stated that he'd been home for lunch at noon and that his wife had been fine then. "I took two containers of raspberries out of the freezer for her because she was going to make a pie."

The postmortem examination had included only a cursory look at the head and throat, and the time of death stipulated marked the husband's statement as a lie. He could not have seen his wife alive and well at noon.

Hardly popular with the M.E., Stovall insisted on further tests, and the contents of the victim's stomach were found to be laced with strychnine poison. That made the case a whole new ball game.

Stovall searched the kitchen shelves above where the woman had fallen, and found an old container of poison on the top shelf. A check of sales on strychnine in the Salem area showed that four and a half pounds of the stuff had been sold in the previous twelve months—all in minute amounts sold from a dozen different outlets.

The husband, more bewildered than ever, was given a polygraph test and passed it cleanly. He did remember buying some rat poison many years before, but had forgotten it was even in the house.

"That poor woman killed herself," Stovall says. "Witnesses said she'd been slipping back into her old depression. She had time enough to take the poison, rinse out the glass, and replace the container on the high shelf. Then convulsions seized her and she fell, striking her head on the sharp kitchen counter. Strychnine kills from sheer exhaustion from the constant convulsions. The throat hemorrhages were caused by convulsive spasms, not from strangulation. And when death is caused by a convulsive disorder, rigor is accelerated. She *was* alive at noon—just as her husband said."

A grand jury overturned the murder charge and ruled the woman's death a suicide.

Jim Stovall keeps a constant reminder of the need for attention to forensic detail in solving crimes above his desk, but *beneath* his desk he keeps a pair of ski boots. That is his avocation and his passion away from the police department. A skier for thirty-five years, he is a member of the Professional Ski Instructors of America—teaching skiing in Oregon and also in Colorado during his vacations. His whole family skis. Today his daughter is a ski instructor, and his son is a skier and a lawyer.

In 1970 Jim Stovall was named *Master Detective*'s

National Police Officer of the Month, and singled out by *Parade* magazine for an honorable mention in their annual salute to the ten most outstanding police officers in America.

He would never have a case more challenging than the one that began in earnest on November 26, 1968—exactly ten months after the disappearance of Linda Slawson. The second case was part of a pattern, but a pattern with too few variables yet known to be apparent. But the serial killer is never satiated. He kills and moves on to kill again and again, until something stops him. He choreographs his killing so carefully, remembering which of his deadly steps succeed and incorporating them into his pattern.

And in so doing, he leaves, for the men who know what to look for, a path as plain as a trail of bread crumbs.

5

By the fall of 1968 Jerry Brudos had found a job, again as an electrician, for a firm south of Salem. Not a great job—but a job. His marriage was still intact, but it was strained. Darcie had cooled to his sexual advances; she did not often refuse him, but he sensed she found him disgusting. She was away from their home so much now, spending four days a week with two sisters who were her good friends.

He still ruled the home with an iron hand, however. He told Darcie that the shop area was his and that he didn't want her going out to the garage without his permission. He got a strong padlock and put it on the door to assure that he would have privacy. She complained some because the freezer was out there, and he said flatly, "Just tell me what you want for supper and I'll get it out of the freezer for you. I don't want you butting into my darkroom when I'm working— you'll ruin everything if you do."

He didn't worry so much about her poking around in the attic. He told her that he'd seen mice and rats up there, and that scared her. He had his treasures up there, boxes of shoes and bras and slips, all sizes. Some were even large enough for him to slip into himself to spend hours enjoying the feel of the soft cloth against his bare skin. The things were his, and he didn't want Darcie touching them or asking him questions about where he'd got them.

He didn't even like to have her come home unexpectedly from her silly visits to her friends. "You call me before you come home," he told her. "I like to have some warning who's going to pop in on me."

"But I'm your *wife*," she protested.

"You just call, like I told you."

There was no point in arguing with him. She did call, but that didn't seem to be enough. Jerry flooded her friends with calls of his own whenever she was away from home. "He wanted to know where I was, what I was doing, when I was coming home. He was terribly jealous of me, wondering who I was with—and I never was with anyone but my girlfriends. Once I asked him why he was always checking on me, why I couldn't come back to my own house without calling first. He made a joke of it. He said he wanted to be sure he got the blond out of the house before I got there."

He had never cheated on her, not as far as she knew. It was a dumb joke. She was a little afraid of him now, because he seemed so strange. He had never harmed her physically, but he was so big, and even his friends said he was the strongest human they'd ever seen. He could carry a refrigerator all by himself and never even show the strain.

Jerry Brudos had begun his fantasy about capturing women when he was seventeen. By the time he was twenty-nine, he had refined it and polished it until it had grown to something right out of Krafft-Ebing, a nightmare of sadism.

He wanted to find someplace where he could set up an underground "butcher shop." It would have cells where he could keep his captives, and a huge freezer room. When he had it all ready, he would take a bus and go out and round up pretty girls and bring them back to his torture complex. He would choose which ones he wanted for his pleasure. He would shoot them and stab them and beat them and play with them sexually, and no one would be able to find out. When he had them, he would take pictures of them for his collection. When he was finally done with them, he would take them into his freezer room and freeze them in the positions he wanted so that he could keep them forever.

He acknowledged that there were problems with his plan. For one thing, it would take thousands and thousands of dollars to finance such a complex. He had barely enough money to pay rent and buy food. He still had to borrow money from his bitch of a mother and play up to her so he could use her car when he needed it. He was smart enough to earn a lot of money, but he just had bad luck: everybody took advantage of him, and so he worked for peanuts.

Practically, too, he figured that if so many girls turned up missing, somebody would catch on and the cops would start sniffing around.

But it was a plan that always stayed in his mind.

It made him dizzy thinking about it. Sometimes he woke up in the middle of the night feeling dizzy, and he knew it was because of his sexual fantasies. He could end them only by rolling over and having sex with his wife. Now when he made love to her, he felt that he was making love to someone else—to one of his captive women. He knew that it was Darcie, but he had an uncanny sensation that it was not.

He didn't hurt her, and she never knew.

At work, the men kept on with their filthy jokes about women, They thought he was some kind of prude because he no longer bothered to laugh. They treated him like he was nobody; it gave Jerry pleasure to realize what fools most men were.

6

Autumn came to Oregon and all the flowers turned black with frost, everything but the roses. The oak leaves turned yellow and covered the red earth, their branches hung with moss that wafted in the wind like an old woman's hair. And the rains came, weeks on end of steady gray rain that dripped from eaves and trees and pushed the rivers up over their banks. From time to time a violent storm swept in from the Pacific Ocean, and the rain pounded incessantly then against the windows of the gray shake house on Center Street and drummed on the thin roof of the garage workshop.

Thanksgiving was just around the corner, and that meant that Jerry would be spending time with people he detested: his own mother—who would complain that she missed her husband, now long buried, and her favorite son, working a thousand miles away, and Darcie's parents, just as bossy and opinionated as they'd ever been.

The constant rain and the dull job and the holidays coming up made him restless. His headaches were like a hammer pounding in his head, demanding that he leave the crowded house and the whining kids and his wife who didn't seem to respect him the way she once had.

It was hard to find trophies in the winter. Nobody hung wash out on lines because it would never get dry. He had to prowl and watch and go inside to steal underwear.

He had to do something to stop the headaches and the dizziness.

At twenty-three, Jan Susan Whitney was well along in preparing for her future goals. She was almost finished with her degree at the University of Oregon in Eugene, some sixty miles south of Salem. No longer attending college full-time, she now lived in McMinnville, southwest of Portland. She had her own car, an older model Rambler, and a job and friends in both McMinnville and Eugene.

Jan Susan Whitney was a pretty girl with short, thick brown hair and blue eyes. She was five feet, seven inches tall and weighed 130 pounds.

She was, perhaps, more trusting than most—or only naive; she occasionally picked up hitchhikers on her trips between Eugene and McMinnville.

On November 26, 1968, Jan concluded a visit to friends in Eugene and headed north on the I-5 freeway toward her apartment in McMinnville. She was dressed in black bell-bottom slacks and a green jacket when she said good-bye to her friends. She planned to be home that evening; it was only a short drive, two hours at most.

Thanksgiving was two days away, and Jan had plans to be with friends and relatives. She was happy, and dependable, and intelligent. There was no reason at all—no predictable reason—for her to completely disappear.

And yet, she did vanish that night.

Since she had been in transit, it was almost impossible for investigators to pin down just where she might have vanished, or if she had been taken away against her will. A check of her apartment indicated that she had not returned from her trip to Eugene; mail and papers had stacked up, and dust lay heavy in the small rooms.

Jan Whitney had not called any of her friends or family. She had simply disappeared somewhere along the I-5 corridor.

A description of her car was sent out on the teletypes in Oregon and adjoining states.

The car was found parked in a rest area on the road leading up to the Santiam Pass just north of Albany, Oregon, and slightly east of the I-5. The red-and-white Rambler had no external damage, and it was locked.

The Oregon state police ordered that the vehicle be

towed into the garages of the Identification Bureau for processing. It was found to have a minor mechanical problem that would preclude its being driven, but there was absolutely no evidence that the driver had been injured in the car.

No blood. No sign of struggle. There were a few personal items belonging to Jan Whitney. There were no keys.

In processing the Rambler, state police I.D. technicians lifted a good latent print from one of its hubcaps. With the technology available in 1968, a single latent print was worthless to detectives unless they had a suspect's print to compare it to. (FBI fingerprint files had single-print information only on the ten most-wanted criminals.)

The discovery of her car in the lonely parking lot made things look ominous for Jan Whitney. She would have no reason to be there on a foggy, dank November evening. If she had left her inoperable car and attempted to walk along the freeway for help, she had not been seen. Since pedestrians along I-5 are quite noticeable because they are so few and far between, it would seem that *someone* reading news stories of her disappearance would have come forward if she had been seen that night. A search of ditches and the land bordering the freeway netted nothing. Not one sign of the missing woman. If she had fallen and been injured, or even killed after being struck by a passing car, she would have been found by the men and dogs that searched.

There seemed to be no ready explanation for the fact that her car was found in the parking lot at the foot of the Santiam Pass. Jan Whitney had been headed for McMinnville, and a detour toward the pass made no sense. Yet her car was there. Why?

Jan Whitney was gone, just as inexplicably as Linda Slawson had disappeared in Portland ten months to the day earlier.

Thanksgiving came two days after Jan Whitney vanished. Jerry Brudos took his family away for the holidays to visit friends and family. While they were gone, there was an accident. A car went out of control on Center Street, sliding on rain-slick streets and crashing into Brudos' garage workshop, damaging the structure and punching a hole in the exterior wall. The Salem police investigated the accident, but they could not get into the garage to estimate the damage because the doors were all locked.

When the family returned, Jerry was agitated to see that there was a hole in the wall of his private workshop. He told Darcie he would take care of some things and then call the police.

A few hours later, he contacted the Salem police accident investigator who had left a card and unlocked the garage so that the officer could check the damage from the inside. When this was accomplished, Jerry nailed boards over the splintered wood and the workshop was completely closed off again.

Jerry was away from home that night for some time, but Darcie didn't think much of it; he was often gone for hours, and he never explained where he had been when he returned.

The Oregon State Police continued their probe into the mysterious disappearance of Jan Whitney, but all the man-hours of work netted exactly nothing.

Oregon State Police Lieutenant Robert White attempted to trace the anonymous correspondent who had mailed a letter from Albany. Sent in a plain envelope, and tediously printed as if the writer wished to disguise his handwriting, the letter said the writer had been at the Santiam rest stop where Miss Whitney's Rambler was abandoned, and, more startling, indicated that he had been present when Jan Whitney disappeared.

Lieutenant White appealed to the public, asking the informant to come forward. But that was the end of it. If the writer was telling the truth, he chose for his own reasons to remain silent. He might have gleaned his information from newspaper accounts of the missing woman, or he might have had actual knowledge, either as a witness or as a perpetrator. There was no way of telling.

Jerry Brudos continued to commute to his job at

Lebanon, Oregon—a tiny hamlet just east of the I-5 freeway—beyond the Albany exit.

Christmas came, and the new year, and Jerry Brudos celebrated his thirtieth birthday. His headaches had improved for a while, but then he felt nervous again and they returned worse than before.

Darcie thought about leaving him. But she had no skills to get a job, and there was no money, and she did not believe in divorce.

7

Jan Whitney had been missing for four months when spring came again to the Willamette Valley. Linda Slawson had been gone for fourteen months. They had disappeared fifty miles apart, and there were not enough similarities between the two cases to allow law officers to connect them. The girls were both young and slender, and attractive—but one apparently had vanished from the streets of Portland, and the other from the freeway south of Salem. At any given time, there is always a handful of women who have disappeared in a metropolitan area. Most have chosen to leave for their own reasons, and eventually return or at least contact their families.

Some do not. Stephanie Vilcko, sixteen, had left her Portland-area home to go swimming in July 1968—and never returned. Stephanie's disappearance came to a tragic denouement on March 18, 1969. A Forest Grove high-school teacher discovered her skeletonized body along the banks of Gales Creek five miles northwest of Forest Grove. By the time she was found, the ravages of time and weather had obliterated tissue that might have told forensic pathologists how she had died. Wind, ice, and water had also carried away any shred of physical evidence left by a killer—if, indeed, there was a killer.

Stephanie, Linda, and Jan were only three among a dozen or more such cases. There had been headlines when the women first vanished, and then column-long articles on back pages of area papers, and finally, small items from time to time. In police departments, the files on the missing and dead women were growing thicker. Cases which detectives wryly refer to as "losers" are always thicker and more complex than the "winners"; they may slip from the public's mind—but they are never, never forgotten by the men who work through one frustrating false lead after another.

Thursday, March 27, 1969, was a typical example of spring in Salem, Oregon; the daffodils around the courthouse were in bloom, along with the earliest rhododendrons and azaleas, but they were alternately buffeted by rainy winds and warmed by a pale sun washing down through the cool air.

Karen Sprinker, nineteen years old and a freshman at Oregon State University in Corvallis, was enjoying a short vacation between terms and had come home to Salem to visit her parents. Her father was a prominent veterinarian in Salem, and Karen had elected to follow him into the field of medicine, although she planned to treat human patients. She was carrying a heavy premed schedule at Oregon State, and earning top grades.

Karen was beautiful, but not in a sultry way; she embodied the sweetness and warmth of an innocent young woman. In an age when chastity was becoming old-fashioned, Karen Sprinker was a virgin, confident in her own principles. She had thick, almost black hair that fell below her shoulders and tumbled across her high forehead in waving bangs. Her eyes were dark brown, and her smile was wide and trusting.

She had never had a reason not to trust.

Karen had graduated from Sacred Heart Academy in Salem in the class of 1968. She was class salutatorian, a member of the National Honor Society, a National Merit Scholarship finalist, winner of the Salem Elks' Leadership Award, and a member of the Marion County Youth Council. With her intelligence and concern for people, she was a natural as a future doctor. All things being equal, she would be practicing by 1979, a full-fledged M.D. before she was thirty.

Shortly before noon on March 27, Karen Sprinker headed for the Meier and Frank Department Store in Salem. She was to meet her mother for lunch in the store's restaurant, and then the two of them were going to shop for spring clothes that Karen could take back to school.

Meier and Frank's is the biggest department store in Salem, located in the downtown area. It is a block and a half east of what were the Salem Police Department's offices in 1969; it is a block and a half north of the Marion County sheriff's offices in the basement of the courthouse. The store complex contains its own many-tiered inside parking garage, a nicety for shoppers, who can avoid walking through the rain that is a definite possibility from November until June.

Mrs. Sprinker waited in the luncheon room for Karen, who was driving her own car. Their lunch date was set for twelve, and Karen was unfailingly prompt. At twelve-fifteen Karen's mother looked at her watch, puzzled. She waved the menu away and asked for a cup of coffee, trying to concentrate on the models wending their way through the crowded room while they showed the store's new outfits.

At twelve-thirty she began to watch the door for sight of her daughter. People nearby finished their meals, and new groups sat down. And still Karen didn't appear. Her mother wondered if there had been some mistake about the time. No, she was sure Karen had understood.

Mrs. Sprinker left the restaurant and found a pay phone nearby. She called the family home, but no one answered. She went back to the lunchroom, but Karen still hadn't arrived. At length she left a message with the hostess, asking her to tell Karen that her mother had gone home—and would be there waiting for a call.

Karen wasn't at home. Everything there was just as Mrs. Sprinker had left it. Karen wasn't at her father's clinic, nor had she called there.

Karen Sprinker's parents went through all the steps that worried parents take when a dependable, thoughtful child cannot be found. If Karen had been an unpredictable girl, or a rebellious girl, it would have been much less frightening. But Karen had always been the kind of daughter who called home if she was going to be even fifteen minutes late. She was happy with her life and with her family. She loved college, and she'd been looking forward to the shopping trip, to the chance for some girl talk with her mother.

The Sprinkers called all of Karen's friends—and none of them had seen or heard from her. All of them were as puzzled as the Sprinkers, stressing that Karen had no problems that her parents might not have been aware of.

Her mother was aware that Karen had been in her menstrual period, and wondered if perhaps she had suddenly been seized with severe cramps, or even if she might have fainted. She had never had unusually severe periods, but there was always the possibility that she had become ill. Her parents called Salem hospitals to see if she might have been admitted.

None of the hospital admitting records listed Karen Sprinker. No illness. No accident.

Reluctantly going to the police—because that step seemed to mark Karen's disappearance as something so much more ominous—the Sprinkers reported Karen as missing.

The Salem police tried to reassure Karen's parents; they had seen so many "missing" people come back with reasonable explanations of why they were gone. Teenagers, particularly, tend to walk away of their own accord. They often have secrets their parents do not suspect, or romances that they think their parents won't approve of. Because they have never been parents, they cannot understand the worry that results when they are late getting home.

The officer taking the complaint urged the Sprinkers to try to remember something that Karen might have said, some hint she might have given about something she planned to do or someplace she wanted to go.

"Could she have gone back to her dorm at Oregon State?"

"No," her mother said impatiently. "I've already called. She hasn't been back since the term ended. Her room is locked."

As the Sprinkers painted a picture of their daughter's habits and her consideration for others, the officer felt a chill. *This* girl didn't sound at all like a runaway. She didn't sound like a girl who might suddenly decide to get married or take off with a boyfriend.

In almost any police department in America, the policy is not to take a formal complaint on a missing adult for twenty-four hours—simply because most of the missing come back within that period. If there are signs of foul play, then of course the search is begun immediately. The reason for the twenty-four-hour delay is pragmatic. There is not enough manpower even in a big police department to look for everyone; there would be no time for other police business. Missing-persons detectives can concentrate only on cases that deal with true vanishings. If a child is missing or if there are indications that the missing person has come to harm, the twenty-four-hour limit is forgotten.

A preliminary report was taken, listing "Karen Elena Sprinker—missing since 12:30 hours, March 27, 1969. Meier and Frank (?)" Then the Sprinkers went home to sit by the phone, to listen for the sound of Karen coming through the front door.

They waited all night long, without any word from Karen.

Salem police went to the parking garage at Meier and Frank, on the off-chance that Karen had come to the store but for some reason had not appeared for her date at the restaurant. They searched through the levels of the parking garage and found no sign of the missing girl, nor signs of anything unusual in the shadows of the looming concrete ramp that wound around and up.

Not until they reached the roof. And there they found Karen Sprinker's car, parked neatly between the diagonal lines of a parking slot, and locked. There was no way to tell how long it had been there; Meier and Frank puts no time limit on shoppers' parking.

Like Jan Whitney's car, there was nothing about it that was out of the ordinary. Some of Karen's books were on the seat, but otherwise it contained nothing. When it was hauled in for processing, technicians at the lab found no blood and no semen on the seat covers or the door panels. There were no cigarettes in the ashtray, and the latent prints lifted from the steering wheel, dashboard, and other surfaces were only those of the Sprinker family.

Whatever had happened to Karen Sprinker had not happened in the car itself.

Scores of shoppers parked on the roof floor every day, and they had only to walk down a flight of concrete stairs to reach a door into the store itself. A matter of a few minutes. Karen had come to the store in broad daylight. That figured, because she was to meet her mother at noon. It would seem to be one of the safest spots in the city of Salem.

But the investigators, led by Jim Stovall, hunkered down and checked the floor from the missing girl's car, down the steps, and all the way to the door for signs of something, anything she might have dropped—even drops of blood.

The parking garage was empty of shoppers now, and while they worked, their own voices echoed as they bounced off the gray walls, making what had been a normal, secure place seem somehow eerie.

"You know," one of the detectives said slowly, "as close as these stairs are to the store entrance, they could be a lonely spot if a young woman happened to be the only one at a given moment who was leaving the parking area. That door into the store is heavy—it would take a little muscle, a little concentration to open it. For those few moments, a woman would be terribly vulnerable."

"Yeah," another responded. "It wouldn't do much good to scream. The traffic noises below, and the hubbub of the store inside—nobody could hear through the door, and nobody could hear on the street. If there wasn't anyone else on the roof to help . . ."

Their musings produced terrible pictures in their minds—remembering the photograph of the slender, smiling girl.

Karen Sprinker's disappearance became the prime case for Jim Stovall and his fellow detectives. Stovall's own daughter was only two years older than Karen, and he knew too well what her family was going through.

The Salem *Capital Journal* and the Salem *Statesman*

carried Karen Sprinker's picture with the question "Have you seen this girl?" under it, and the public responded. There were the usual crank letters and the usual informants who really knew nothing but wanted to espouse theories that sounded good to them. Most of the tips were totally useless, but all leads had to be followed, because one of them might have been vital.

One early lead seemed promising. A Southern Pacific Railroad ticket agent called Salem police to say that he'd seen a girl who looked "just like Karen Sprinker" leave Salem by train for San Francisco. "There were two men with her, and she didn't act like she was afraid of them, but you never can tell. She might have been afraid to ask for help."

The Salem papers printed the information the agent had called in, and almost immediately a Mount Angel man called police to say that the girl on the train had been *his* daughter, who was also a brunette with pretty brown eyes. "She's okay. She's safe in California, and she was traveling with family friends."

A service-station owner who had lived on the Oregon coast contacted Stovall's office to say he was sure he'd sold gas to Karen Sprinker. "She gave me a credit card to pay for the gas, and I'm almost positive the name was Sprinker.

Stovall and Lieutenant "Hap" Hewett left at once for the Oregon coast, but when they got to the station, the owner said he had sent the credit-card slip routinely into the company's home office in Tulsa, Oklahoma. He had mailed it off before he'd read about Karen Sprinker in the newspaper.

The detectives contacted the home office of the oil company, and the personnel there were most cooperative. They went through thousands of credit slips, looking for the one allegedly signed by Karen Sprinker in Oregon. "They finally found one from that station," Stovall recalls. "But the name was Spiker, not Sprinker."

A motorcyclist notified Hewett and Stovall that he had picked up a hitchhiker near Tigard, Oregon, and given her a ride on his Harley. "She had long black hair, and she said she was from Salem."

"Where'd you take her?" Stovall asked.

"She wanted to go to some hippie place in Portland—that commune out by Portland State U. So I took her."

Stovall pulled out a picture of Karen Sprinker. "Is this the girl?"

The biker studied the photograph, and then handed it back with a shrug. "Maybe . . . maybe not. It looks kinda like the chick I picked up. I meet a lotta chicks, and it's kind of hard to tell, you know?"

That Karen Sprinker would have been hitchhiking or that she had any aspirations toward living in a hippie commune seemed unfathomable—but then, the fact that she was still missing was just as hard to understand. Anything was possible.

Karen's boyfriend was anxious to pursue any avenue that might help him find the young woman. He went to Portland, dressed in jeans and a batik shirt, his beard deliberately unshaven. He wanted to look like a hippie, and he succeeded. For several days he loitered around hippie hangouts, blending into the rough crowd until people there got used to him. He asked carefully casual questions, and mentioned he was looking for his "old lady who split on me."

Sitting in dark rooms that smelled of marijuana, eating sprouts and brown rice, and listening to babies cry in counterpoint to rock music, Karen's friend knew she wouldn't be comfortable in this counterculture, but he wanted so badly to find her and take her home safe to her family.

In the end, he gave it up. Karen was gone, and no one knew where—or, if someone knew, no one was telling.

Salem detectives gave the young college student credit for trying and empathized with his frustration: their own efforts weren't producing any solid leads either.

One story reached the Salem Police Department circuitously, and was so bizarre that it might have been dismissed . . . and yet . . .

Two high-school girls in Salem went to a woman they trusted and described a peculiar person they had seen while they were shopping at Meier and Frank a few weeks before Karen Sprinker vanished.

"There was a person in the parking garage," one girl began.

"A *person*?" the woman asked.

"Well, it looked like a woman. I mean, we thought it was a woman at first, but . . ."

"But what?"

"We saw this tall, heavy person. All dressed up with high heels and a dress. 'She' was just standing there in the garage, as if she was waiting for someone. She was tugging at her girdle and fixing her nylons."

"But you don't think it was a woman at all—is that it?"

"Yes!" the other girl said. "The person looked so strange that we drove on up the ramp and came around again. And now we're sure it wasn't a woman at all. It was a man dressed up like a woman!"

The housewife who listened to the girls' story urged them to go to the police.

Men in drag are not terribly unusual; it is sometimes a harmless aberration, but given the circumstances surrounding Karen Sprinker's disappearance, the presence of a huge man in women's clothing in the Meier and Frank parking garage in early March signaled a possible connection.

"Suppose there was a man there, dressed up like a woman," one investigator offered. "Suppose he pretended to be ill, or even called Karen over to ask her a question? She wouldn't be as cautious if she thought it was a woman. She would have walked up to him, never expecting trouble. She was the kind of young woman who would have been eager to help."

"And he could have grabbed her?"

"Yes."

Perhaps that was the way it had happened. Perhaps not. The transvestite incident could have been a random thing, some alumnus of one of the state institutions in Marion County, some frightened and completely nonviolent man who acted out his kinkiness by waltzing around Meier and Frank in a dress and spike heels. Store employees did not remember ever seeing such a creature.

Whatever had happened, Karen Sprinker never came

home. Good Friday passed, and then Easter, and classes began again at Oregon State University, but Karen wasn't there to join her friends. Sadly her family cleared out her room in Callahan Hall in Corvallis. Everything Karen had owned—her books, records, treasured photos, clothes—everything had been left behind except for the green skirt and sweater she'd worn on March 27, and her purse.

By the third week in April, there was so little to hope for. Karen's body had not been found, so there was still the faintest of chances that she might have suffered an injury or illness that had brought on amnesia. Not knowing was the worst of all; there was the possibility that she was being held captive somewhere, unable to call home.

Karen Sprinker's picture was tacked over Jim Stovall's desk—a reminder in front of him always that she waited, somewhere, for someone to come and find her. He had never known Karen, but it almost seemed that he had; he had learned so much about her, admired all the accomplishments and ambitions in a girl so young, that she was far more to him than a picture on a wall.

It is always that way with good detectives. They come to know the victims of the crimes they investigate as well as their own families. And knowing, they are driven to avenge them.

— 8 —

Darcie Brudos read about the disappearance of Karen Sprinker; there was no way to avoid it unless you didn't read the papers and never watched television. She found it quite frightening, and she discussed it with her women friends. She didn't worry about herself so much, but she was concerned about Megan, and she watched her little girl carefully while she played in the yard. She took her to school and picked her up each day. Meier and Frank's store was less than a mile from their house, just west down Center Street several blocks and then a few blocks north.

The papers were hinting that there was a maniac loose, suggesting that whatever had happened to Karen Sprinker might happen to someone else if the person wasn't caught. Darcie wouldn't go out at night by herself any longer, and she kept the doors and windows tightly locked when Jerry was gone.

He was gone a lot. Working in Lebanon during the day, except for when his headaches were too bad. And then he had so many errands to run, and auto parts to buy—the ones he found by rummaging through junkyards in Portland and Salem. Sometimes he went to Corvallis; he occasionally did yard work for a friend over there. She had no idea where Jerry went most of the time, and it annoyed him when she asked.

He was getting even more obsessed with privacy in his workshop. If she rapped on the door to try to get in to check what was in the freezer, it seemed to make him angrier than ever. He always said he would get what she wanted, but that was inconvenient because she wasn't always sure what food was left. Sometimes she just wanted to have the chance to stand there and see what was in the freezer and hope it would give her an idea for supper.

Jerry had been upset when she'd found the door to his darkroom open one day and walked in after checking to be sure the light was on. She'd gone out to the garage to do the laundry and thought she'd just peek in at Jerry and say "Hi."

There were trays of developing solution on the counter, and she looked idly at the pictures he was printing. And then she gasped with surprise when she saw that the pictures were of women. Nude women.

"Jerry? What are these?" she blurted.

He smiled and moved quickly in front of the counter so that her view was blocked. "Those? Nothing. Just some film a kid from the college asked me to develop for him. I didn't know what they were until they turned out. Just kid stuff. I'll tell him not to bring that kind of pictures around anymore."

She didn't know whether to believe him or not, but then she thought about the way Jerry was. He was pretty bashful around any woman but herself, and she couldn't imagine him taking nude pictures himself— not of anyone but her.

"Okay. But don't let Megan see those pictures. Get them back to the guy."

Jerry promised that he would, and she promised that she wouldn't barge into his workshop again.

"Use the intercom, Darcie. That's easier. Just tell me what you want, and I'll get it for you."

Darcie sighed. It was easier not to argue with him. He had always been different, a little out of step with the rest of the people she knew—but all her friends had complaints about their husbands too. It seemed to be a matter of accepting the things you didn't like about your mate and trying to work around them. She knew he was unhappy with her own growing independence. Independence. She had to smile at that. She had so little freedom, really. With the kids to look after, and having to report to Jerry all the time, every minute of her days and nights was accounted for.

There were other things that Darcie Brudos tried not to think about. She hadn't seen Jerry in women's clothing since he'd put on the bra and girdle, but she'd found some pictures that upset her. Jerry had left them lying around—either carelessly or deliberately.

She recognized that it was Jerry in the pictures, but it was the Jerry who liked to dress up in women's underclothes. In one he lay on his back on their bed, holding a pillow over his face in a clumsy attempt to hide his features. He wore a white bra—it had to be a 48 C at least—and a long-line panty girdle, also white, stockings, and those same black highheels. Where on earth could he have found them? He wore size 13 shoes.

Another picture was almost the same, only Jerry was lying flat on his stomach, with his left arm draped over the edge of the bed, his right arm tucked beneath his "breasts," and his head turned to the right. Then there was one where he wore a black slip, trimmed with black lace, and those same shoes. She wondered who might have taken them, and then realized that he'd probably photographed himself. He had a thirty-five-millimeter camera that had a remote-control attachment. Once, when they were traveling, he had posed all four of them in front of a sign that said "You Are Now Leaving the State of California" and clicked the shutter in his hand. That picture had turned out just fine, so she knew he had the equipment to take pictures that way.

She had shoved the pictures away someplace; she sure didn't want anyone else to see them. He was still always after her for sex, even when she let him know she wasn't interested. If he was a homosexual, she was sure he wouldn't want intercourse with a woman. Men were either gay or they weren't, according to what she knew. It wasn't something she could discuss with her girlfriends; that would be a betrayal of Jerry, and anyway, it made her ashamed.

Whenever Darcie managed to put her worries out of her mind, it seemed that something else happened to bring them all back. Sometime after she'd found the pictures, she found a "thing"—she couldn't quite figure out what it was. It was round and heavy, a few inches in diameter, and it seemed to be made of some

kind of plastic. She had held it and turned it over, and
then realized that it looked just like a woman's breast—
not as large, but almost a perfect replica.

"What is this, Jerry?" she'd asked.

"That? That's just an idea I had to make a paperweight."

"A *breast*?"

"For a novelty item. Kind of a joke."

"It looks so real."

"Yeah." He took the mold from her. "Well, it
didn't work. I put too much hardener in the plastic."

She had to go way back in their relationship to
remember when Jerry had told jokes that were really
funny. All of his "jokes" now had a sexual or a hostile
tone. He seemed either angry with her or disappointed
in her. She vowed that she would try to be nicer to
him, dress up more in the fancy clothes he liked on
her, and try to be more loving.

If she only tried harder, she thought their marriage
might get better.

— 9 —

On Wednesday, April 23, 1969, Karen Sprinker had been missing for three weeks and six days, and the Salem police had virtually run out of new leads. Forty-seven miles north of Salem, in Portland, the news of the Sprinker disappearance had never been headlined, and it is doubtful that Linda Salee of that city had ever heard of Karen Sprinker.

And yet Linda Salee was about to become part of a dread sisterhood.

Linda Dawn Salee was twenty-two years old, a tiny woman who stood only five feet, one inch tall. But she was one of those feisty, bouncy little women who excel at athletics. She was really quite strong and wonderfully coordinated; she had a shelf full of bowling trophies to prove it.

Linda Salee was also exceptionally pretty. She had ash-blond hair which she wore in the teased pompadour style so popular in the late sixties. Her eyes were blue and fringed with improbably long lashes, and her smile revealed perfect teeth. Indeed, Linda's smile was so outstanding that she had won a "Miss Smile" contest a few years back.

Like Linda Slawson, Jan Whitney, and Karen Sprinker, Linda Salee was so attractive that she always drew appreciative male stares. She had a boyfriend whom she loved and she wasn't interested in other men at all.

Linda worked days in the offices of Consolidated Freightways in Portland, and she left work at four-thirty P.M. on April 23. She planned to drive to the huge shopping mall at Lloyd Center and shop for presents for her boyfriend's birthday. Then she was going to go to the Eastside YMCA for a swim in the pool there, where her boyfriend was a lifeguard. They were both interested in sports and in physical fitness, just one of the many things they shared in common. Since she worked days and he worked evenings, the only way they could see each other during the week was for Linda to come to the pool and swim.

Linda drove her own car, her pride and joy—a bright red Volkswagen Bug—to Lloyd Center and parked it carefully on the sixth floor of the parking garage. She wore a beige coat against the cold that belied the fact that spring had begun officially more than a month earlier.

Because she was in love and because she was a young woman of generous spirit, Linda spent a lot of money on presents for her boyfriend. Her original plan had been to get him a leather watchband. She went to a jewelry shop first and the clerk there remembered her well. It was a slow period in the day, and she took a long time making up her mind. She finally made a selection, and headed for a men's clothing store.

Again, the clerk who waited on her remembered her. She was so pretty, and so careful about her shopping. She bought her friend a blue suedecloth jacket and a pair of walking shorts. As she left the men's store, the clerk glanced at the clock on the wall and noted that it was five-fifteen P.M.

She sat on one of the benches provided for tired shoppers and opened the small sack that held the watchband. Seeing it in the bright lights overhead, she decided it wasn't the right color after all. She walked back to the jewelry shop and apologized to the clerk. "I'm sorry. It's not what he wanted. Could I return it?"

Her money was refunded, and Linda smiled at the clerk and left the shop, headed for the parking garage.

At the YMCA pool, Linda Salee's boyfriend watched over the shouting, leaping kids in the water. He had to keep a close eye on them. The adult swimmers were content to do their laps doggedly, get it over with, and head for the showers. The kids were another story altogether; if you didn't watch them, they'd run on the decks, cannonball off the board without looking for swimmers below, or attempt to venture into the deep end of the pool when they couldn't swim well enough to manage it. He sat on his perch high above the pool and scanned the water constantly, his nose itching from the chlorine fumes that permeated the air. Sometimes Linda could emerge from the women's locker room and sneak up on him before he noticed her. Her light touch on his toes always made him jump—and made him happy too. She was a dynamite-looking girl, and he was proud to see her swimming in the pool and know that she was *his* girl.

It was cold outside, and rainy, and the temperature outside, combined with the fumes in the pool, steamed up the glass face of the wall clock. The young lifeguard looked at it and realized it was after seven o'clock. He looked at the clock again to be sure it was that late, and it was. Almost seven-thirty.

Linda should have arrived an hour ago. Where was she?

The kids' swim session was over, and an "Adults Only" session began. With a spate of time when he didn't have to guard so closely, Linda's boyfriend watched the door of the women's locker room. There were more men than women always, and on this Wednesday night, only a few women drifted out, tucking their hair under their caps. A couple of overweight gals over forty who were determined to slim down. The tall woman who came every night, rain or shine, and swam as if she'd once been a champion. A few teenagers who giggled and paddled around the shallow end.

Linda never showed up.

Her friend changed into his street clothes when the last swimmer was out of the pool, and drove to her apartment. His knocking went unanswered and he was a little angry with her—but only for a few minutes. He knew her too well to think she would have stood him up. She had been excited about his birthday and had teased him about all the presents he was going to get. Even now, standing in the empty hall outside her apartment, he half-expected to see her jump out and yell, "Surprise!"

When Linda Salee didn't arrive at her job at Consolidated Freightways the next morning, her friends and family grew frantic for her safety. There was simply no explanation but that she was someplace from which she was unable to come home.

Oregon state police investigators, aware of the other cases involving missing young women, treated Linda Salee's disappearance very seriously. With the information that she had intended to go shopping in Lloyd Center, they joined detectives from Portland in a search of the grounds and parking garage.

It was like a replay of Karen Sprinker's case. Linda Salee's car was located in the parking garage. It too was locked and there were no indications that a struggle had taken place in or around the vehicle.

There was no conclusion to be drawn other than that someone had taken Linda away against her will.

Comparing the cases of the missing women, detectives in Oregon saw similarities again and again. Four pretty young women had disappeared from the mainstream of life within sixteen months, leaving no clues at all behind. All the girls had vanished within a fifty-mile area. None of them had anything in her background that would have made her a likely candidate to run away. There were no witnesses. There were no bits of physical evidence—not a piece of clothing, a dropped purse, a shoe. Not even a brush of blood or a hair. Not one of them had reported to friends or police that she had reason to be afraid because of an insistent suitor or an obscene phone call.

That meant that the Oregon investigators were looking for the most elusive kind of suspect, someone who snatched victims by random choice. Someone had apparently watched until he saw women who appealed to whatever obsession drove him. And then he had stalked them until he found them in places where they could not call for help. Whatever ruse or device he had used to get them, he had done it quickly and silently.

They were gone.

It almost seemed as if the person who had taken them away had deliberately chosen victims from areas patrolled by different police agencies. Linda Slawson from the jurisdiction of the Portland city police, Jan Whitney from the I-5 freeway, policed by the Oregon State Police and Linn County Sheriff's officers, Karen Sprinker from the city of Salem, and Linda Salee from the city of Portland again.

Whoever had taken them—and it had to be assumed that it was a male, and not a woman responsible—he was devious and clever.

But not clever enough. Communication between law-enforcement agencies is essential, and when a major case occurs, every agency within a prescribed area becomes aware of it. Something terrible was happening in northern Oregon, something that posed a threat to pretty young women, and bulletins and teletypes flooded every law-enforcement agency in the region. Descriptions of the missing girls and the circumstances of their disappearances were sent to the thirteen western states via teletype.

Lane County detectives in Eugene, Oregon, forty-four miles south of Salem, watched the developments of the missing girls' cases closely. They had an unsolved homicide case whose victim resembled the other women. Mrs. Janet Shanahan, twenty-two, had been found strangled in the trunk of her car, the vehicle abandoned on a Eugene street only a day after Linda Salee vanished.

Janet Shanahan fit the victim profile quite closely; the M.O. was different, however, in that her body had been found. But in trying to figure a phantom killer's M.O., this was a significant break in the pattern. Further, the other women had disappeared in time periods that were at least a month apart. That, too, stamped the Shanahan case as outside the pattern.

Whatever the answer was, lawmen moved with speed. They did not want to think that, when the end of May approached, there would be another abduction—that still another young woman would fall prey to the faceless marauder who seemed to rove at will through their territory, picking off one beautiful victim after another.

— 10 —

The Long Tom River is a narrow tributary that branches off the powerful Willamette River some twelve miles south of Corvallis. It wends its way south for twenty-four miles and finally empties into the Fern Ridge Reservoir just west of Eugene. Rushing between banks choked with thick underbrush, the Long Tom is an excellent river to fish—for those who know the prime spots. Except for the hamlets of Monroe and Cheshire, there are no towns close to the Long Tom; it is a country river, and hardly known to those who don't live in the area where it flows. In places it is grand and picturesque, but in other spots the Long Tom is as lonely and bleak as a ghost river.

Until 1961 the Irish Bend Road crossed the Long Tom through an ancient covered bridge, one of the few still standing in the Northwest. The weathered structure is reminiscent of the covered bridges in Pennsylvania and New England. By 1961 modern vehicles found the passage through the old bridge far too tight a squeeze, and a new concrete bridge was built parallel to the old—but preservationists insisted that the old Bundy Bridge be saved. And so it remained in 1969, a relic of the past whose foundations nudged the new bridge crossing—no longer functional for anything but to give shelter to fishermen when the wind wailed along the river and rain dripped down the brims of their hats.

The Bundy Bridge site is one of the busiest along the river, but in comparison to city rivers, it is still a quiet spot. In winter and early spring the Long Tom creeps high up on the pillars that support the new bridge, full of rain and melted-snow runoff from mountains and foothills.

By May 10 the river had fallen back, and lapped listlessly at the double quintet of concrete pillars. A man could stand close to shore now and the water would reach only his waist. Old timbers caught on naked saplings and choked the shallows, looking like sea creatures drawn from the bottom. But the bank vegetation had begun to green, and there were a few spring daisies and wild irises brightening the weeds there.

A lone fisherman parked his truck on the Irish Bend Road that Saturday and gathered his gear for an afternoon of fishing. The sky was leaden and full of clouds that lowered overhead and threatened to burst and spill their substance at any moment. No matter; neither fish nor fishermen mind rain.

The angler walked onto the Bundy Bridge and peered down into the muddied water. He shivered involuntarily as a sudden gust of wind pulled at his jacket. He watched a flight of water birds lift off the far shore and wing downstream, and thought how deserted the Long Tom seemed. An occasional car had swept by on the road, but when the traffic disappeared, it seemed as if he could hear every crackle in the brush along the bank.

He hunched his shoulders and turned back to the river, looking for a good spot to drop his line. He didn't want to get it caught on one of the tree snags and spend a half-hour getting disentangled.

The current caught his lure and tugged it downstream. He cast again, farther out.

And then he saw something.

A large bulky object floated just beneath the surface of the Long Tom, twisting lazily in the drift, but caught by something that held it fast. It wasn't a log; it seemed too soft for that, and yet too solid to be only a bundle of cloth. He watched it idly, and felt an odd prickling at the back of his neck.

The fisherman laid his pole carefully on the bank and sidestepped down, placing his feet tentatively in the damp weeds. He caught onto a maple sapling and hung out over the river to get a closer look.

He saw, but could not compute what he saw for a moment or two—and then he reeled back in horror, almost losing his footing and plunging into the Long Tom himself. The object in the river was a human being. He could see fine light hair fan out and undulate in the river's flow, and caught a glimpse of pale flesh.

He did not wait to see if it was a man or a woman caught in the river, or even to wonder how the body had come to be there. He was up the bank in three leaps, and headed for his truck.

The call came in to the Benton County sheriff's office, and Sheriff Charles E. Reams dispatched deputies to the Long Tom River. The deputies radioed back that the presence of a body in the Long Tom had been confirmed. It was that of a young woman.

"She's been in the river some time," the officer reported. "And she didn't just fall in. The body's weighted down with a car transmission."

The news that a young woman's body had been found was electrifying to detectives in northern Oregon, and investigators in Salem and Portland waited anxiously to hear who she was and how she had died. Since the body had been found in Benton County, the case was technically and legally under the jurisdiction of Sheriff Reams's department, but Reams and Benton County District Attorney Frank Knight were fully aware of the wider ramifications. If this woman proved to be one of the missing women, it would be the first break—however tragic—in the baffling cases.

District Attorney Frank Knight is what lawmen call a "policemen's D.A.," an indefatigable worker who stays with a case from the very beginning. Stovall would voice his admiration for Knight many times over the weeks that followed. "He's the kind of D.A. we most admire—he's with us all the way, always available. If we need legal input in a hurry, he's there. From the moment that first body was found in the Long Tom, Knight was part of the team. He never got in the way of our scene investigations, but he put in as many twenty-four-hour days as the rest of us did."

The road leading to the Bundy Bridge was cordoned off, and only lawmen and officials from the Oregon State Medical Examiner's Office were allowed to cross the barriers. Reams and Knight stood by as the girl's body was lifted from the Long Tom and carried up the bank.

It was not an easy task; the deputies who had gone into the river were strong, husky men, but the girl, when weighted down by the transmission, weighed almost two-hundred pounds.

She was a short woman, and quite fair. She had ash-blond hair and blue eyes. They had somehow expected that it would be Karen Sprinker, but it was not. Karen had been taller and was a brunette.

This girl was young too, and the waters of the Long Tom had been cold, preserving her body with the heedless tenderness of nature. A beige coat still clung to the body, but many of her garments were gone— either torn away by the current or deliberately removed by the killer who had put her into the river.

William Brady, Chief Medical Examiner for the State of Oregon, was on his way from Portland, and the body would not be moved until he arrived. In the meantime, Reams sent deputies to canvass the countryside to see if anyone might have seen something or someone dumping a heavy burden into the Long Tom.

It was a fruitless task. The closest farmhouse was a good half-mile from the Bundy Bridge. No nearby resident had seen anything suspicious. It was likely that the disposal of the body had taken place under cover of darkness.

Throughout the day, into the night, and for days following, the bridge over the Long Tom would be the site of intense police investigation.

Dr. William Brady arrived to make a preliminary examination of the dead girl. Brady is one of the foremost forensic pathologists in America, a tall, dapper man who dresses more like a visiting ambassador than a working medical examiner. He eschews the coveralls worn by most investigators at a grisly crime scene, and yet he does his work so deftly that he emerges as immaculate as when he arrives.

Brady came to Oregon from New York City. He was a forensic pathologist in the Manhattan office of the New York City Medical Examiner's Office before he set up the most sophisticated state medical examiner's system in the country. Oregon abolished the coroner system in 1956, and today its medical examiner's system is a model for other states.

Because Oregon is essentially a rural state with the bulk of its population in Portland, Salem, and Eugene, Brady feels that law-enforcement agencies in small communities should have the benefit of the expertise of a state medical examiner. No body may be removed in a suspicious death until removal has been authorized by a deputy medical examiner, and thereafter it is not to be undressed, washed, or otherwise prepared before autopsy.

Too many wrongful deaths go undetected in areas without a medical examiner's system, because once vital physical evidence is lost, it can never be recovered. Too many victims of wrongful death are buried without autopsy, and the killers' secrets are buried with them.

Oregon has never had more than 150 murders in a given year, and only one-third of those merit intense investigation. When that murder rate is compared with statistics of cities like Houston, Miami, and Detroit, Oregon seems a safe place to live.

But not for everyone. Not for the young woman who was transported to Dr. Brady's offices to await autopsy.

The girl was Linda Salee. Detectives had suspected that it was she right from the beginning. Decomposition was moderate; it could not have been Linda Slawson or Jan Whitney. They had been gone too long for visual identification. Someone had taken Linda Salee more than seventy miles away from the Lloyd Center shopping mall, killed her, and then had thrown her away in the Long Tom.

Her killer had made a tactical error. He had either misjudged the depth of the lonely river or had been unable to carry the weighted body out into the center of the river, where the depth was so much greater.

Or perhaps he'd been so cocky that he didn't care if her body was found. Perhaps something in him made him seek discovery of his terrible handiwork.

Linda Salee's body had been bound to the auto transmission with nylon cord and copper wire. A reddish fabric resembling a mechanic's industrial cloth was caught in her bonds. That might prove to be a valuable clue. A mass-produced item certainly, but something that must be saved along with the cord and wire.

The cause of death? Dr. Brady found the classic signs of traumatic asphyxiation. There were the pete-chial hemorrhages (pinpoint hemorrhages) of the strap muscles of the neck, the lungs, the heart, the eyes, that occur when the lungs cannot take in air. The hyoid bone at the back of the tongue, that fragile u-shaped bone, was fractured. There was the broad, flat mark of some kind of ligature around the slender neck.

And, with these signs, there would be a faint bit of comfort for Linda Salee's family. Death by traumatic asphyxiation, by strangling, is quick. Loss of consciousness occurs very rapidly, and death itself follows quietly.

Had Linda Salee been raped? That was impossible to determine. Long immersion in water dilutes any semen that may be present, so that no absolute tests can be made.

There was something else found during the postmortem on Linda Salee, something that would be kept from the media because it was so bizarre and unexplainable at the moment.

Dr. Brady found two needle marks in the victim's rib cage, one on each side, three or four inches below the armpit. The skin surrounding the needle punctures was marked by postmortem burns. Dr. Brady had never seen anything quite like it before.

There were some bruises, some contusions and abrasions. Linda Salee, the spunky little bowler, had fought her killer ferociously. But she had been too tiny and he had won.

*　　*　　*

The activity at the Long Tom River continued throughout the weekend. Reserve sheriff's officers—skilled scuba divers—combed the river from shore to shore and north and south of the Bundy Bridge. A half-dozen of the black-rubber-suited swimmers dived again and again into the muddy river to find . . . what? Perhaps the clothing that was missing when Linda Salee was found. Perhaps her purse. Possibly even something left behind by her killer.

They came up with old tires, junk, and tangled clots of weeds that had felt like cloth in the depths of the water. They grew chilled and exhausted, and still they dived, carefully working the river in a grid pattern, covering every inch of it. It was dangerous, macabre work. Sometimes the divers surfaced and felt the tree snags clutching at them. Sometimes they worked in rat's nests of debris, feeling claustrophobic.

But none of them quit.

What had happened to Linda Salee enraged normal men. Especially police officers. If they could not have saved her, they would now find her killer and hand him over to the judicial system.

On Monday the horror accelerated into nightmare. Fifty feet from where Linda Salee's body had been found, a diver discovered another figure floating beneath the surface. A figure bound to something that held it down.

He headed for the pale light above him and surfaced with a shout, signaling his fellow divers to join him.

There was indeed a second body in the river.

The news was flashed immediately to Salem police headquarters, and Jim Stovall and Salem Detective Jerry Frazier ran for their car and sped toward the Long Tom. They were there when the divers brought up Karen Sprinker.

Karen had been missing for forty-six days. Forty-six days of agony for her parents. Forty-six days of hoping against hope that she might come back to them. With the latest discovery, that hope was gone.

When the divers carried Karen to the banks of the Long Tom, there was no doubt that her death had been similar to Linda Salee's. Her body was weighted down with the head of a six-cylinder engine. It had been lashed to her body with nylon cord and copper wiring like that used to tie the other body to the auto transmission. There was also a red mechanic's cloth tied to the engine head.

The Oregon investigators, working their individual cases—but conferring with one another—had begun to think that the girls' disappearances might be part of a common plan, and had approached their probe that way. But the knowledge that they had been right was more alarming than reassuring; they did, clearly, have a maniac loose in the state, a lust killer, moving undetected, the worst kind of killer because he does not stop killing until either he is apprehended or is himself dead.

Karen Sprinker's body was autopsied by Dr. William Brady, and on preliminary examination the cause of death seemed the same as Linda Salee's: traumatic asphyxiation.

The term "autopsy," loosely defined, means "to find out for oneself." Homicide detectives and forensic pathologists must set their minds on two levels. Their job—and their duty—is to consider their cases scientifically, to maintain a kind of objectivity into which none of their own emotions intrude. If they are not able to suspend feelings, they cannot do their jobs. What they have to cope with is too tragic. Later, when the killer has been caught, they can afford the luxury of rage and tears. While the search for clues is going on, they must be clinical and detached.

It was extremely difficult to be detached about Karen Sprinker, the innocent young woman whose dreams of becoming a doctor had been wiped out by the killer who left her body floating in the Long Tom.

Lieutenant Jim Stovall and Lieutenant Gene Daugherty of the Oregon State Police—who would work closely together in the intense probe that lay ahead— were present at the postmortem examination of Karen Sprinker.

From this point on, Jim Stovall and Gene Daugherty would be the two investigators at the head of the probe into the search for the killer of Linda Salee and Karen Sprinker—and perhaps of other young women still missing. Daugherty, stationed at the Oregon State Police headquarters in Salem, is a big man, well over six feet, muscular, with the sandy hair and ruddy complexion of a true Irishman. Like Stovall, he was one of the best detectives in the state of Oregon. They would work exceptionally well together, sharing a belief in the power of physical evidence and the necessity to find some common denominator that would link a suspect to the crimes. Neither of them would see much of their wives and families for a long time to come. Nor would Jerry Frazier, the dark-haired, compactly built Salem police detective who had been assigned to work with Stovall. Other detectives in many Oregon jurisdictions would be drawn into the probe as it moved inexorably forward, but Daugherty, Stovall, and Frazier would continue to be at its center until the end.

Any reputable pathologist insists that reverence for the dead be maintained during autopsy; although the body must be examined to determine cause of death and to search for possible vital physical evidence, those in attendance never forget that the deceased deserves respect. Dr. Brady is a stickler about this, and Stovall and Daugherty agree with him. The men were silent as Brady began.

Although Karen Sprinker had also succumbed to asphyxiation, the ligature marks left on her neck were somewhat different from those on Linda Salee's throat. In Karen's case, the ligature had been a narrow band— probably a rope. Again, it had been a rapid death; young women do not have the throat musculature to stave off strangulation. And, again, it was small comfort.

Karen Sprinker had been fully clothed when she was discovered in the Long Tom. She wore the green skirt and sweater that her mother had described on the missing-persons report. She wore cotton panties, but, surprisingly, the simple cotton bra she usually wore had been replaced by a waist-length black bra that was far too big for her.

Odd.

The bra could not have been Karen Sprinker's; her

mother had inventoried all of her clothing to see what
was missing when Karen had vanished, and she owned
no underwear such as this. Further, Karen's bra size
was 34 A or B, and this long-line black bra had to be
at least a 38 D.

As Brady removed the brassiere, sodden lumps of
brown paper toweling dropped out.

Karen had no breasts; her killer had removed them
after death.

And then he had fashioned the illusion of breasts by
stuffing the cups of the black brassiere with wadded
paper towels.

There were indications that Karen Sprinker had been
sexually assaulted by her killer, but, again, it was
impossible to tell absolutely because of her long immersion in the river. There were no other obvious
wounds on her body.

The results of the autopsy on Karen Sprinker were
withheld from the press. Again, only the terse "death
by traumatic asphyxiation" was given to the media.

Karen Sprinker and Linda Salee had been stalked
and abducted by a lust killer. Stovall and Daugherty
had little hope that Linda Slawson and Jan Whitney
would ever be found alive. They stood by while the
divers continued their combing of the depths of the
Long Tom, half-expecting a shout of discovery that
meant those girls too were hidden there.

After days, however, the search was suspended.
The river was empty of bodies now, and would give up
nothing more to aid in the investigation.

11

Jerry Brudos read about the discovery of the bodies in the Long Tom River. He was not particularly concerned. The cops didn't know anything, really. The papers weren't telling everything; the cops had to know a few more details than the paper was giving—but not that much more. He had been very careful. He had planned it all well. Actually, he figured the cops had to be pretty stupid. They'd been right there with their noses poking through the hole in his garage, and they hadn't seen anything at all. They'd only thanked him for his time and signed the forms for the insurance claims. He had to smile when he heard Darcie dithering about the dead girls and how frightened she was. Darcie didn't know anything either.

He felt quite magical, and full of power. Well, he'd waited long enough to exert his power, and now, nobody was going to stop him. Not his mother, or his wife, or the police. Not anyone.

Even Darcie was being nicer to him, beginning to do the things that he'd begged her to do for years. He thought she must sense his new confidence, and he loved her more than ever, if possible. She was really the only woman he had ever loved.

Darcie had started taking dancing lessons! Now they would be able to get dressed up and go out dancing together and she would wear high heels and pretty clothes and every man on the dance floor would be jealous because she would dance with no one but him.

All the shrinks over the years had insisted that his thinking wasn't normal, that he needed therapy. He had the last laugh now; his thought processes were as smooth as tumblers in a lock. He could plan and carry

94

out whatever he wanted to do, and it all worked. He didn't need a shrink to tell his troubles to. He didn't need to "grow up," and he didn't have to bow down to anyone.

The thing was that, once he started on one of his prowling plans, and once he had a woman, he was seized with a feeling that what he was doing was right, that there was no need for him to consider if he should stop or go ahead. He just let the fantasy take him over.

He reveled in having control. He could move about at his own whim. The one thing he could not bear was to have someone else decide what he should do and where he should be at any given time. He was in charge of his own destiny. That was important.

Sometimes he still had his dizzy spells and sometimes he still got depressed, an overwhelming black depression that settled over him and made him too sad for words. Then he would begin to wonder why Darcie had waited so long to take dancing lessons. He had asked her to dance with him for years, and she wouldn't. He wondered if it was too late now.

And he couldn't enjoy sex with her the way he once had. It left him feeling empty, and she didn't seem very enthusiastic or satisfied with him. If she knew how strong and important he was, she might be more sensual. But he couldn't tell her; she might not understand.

Damn. That forced him to remember his failures. Before the short little girl at Lloyd Center, he had struck out twice. It made him feel bad to think about it.

He had to think about his few failures; he needed to evaluate what had gone wrong and correct it. There was that blonde bitch in Portland. He was still furious with her.

On the twenty-first of April, Jerry had gone to the parking garage at Portland State University to look for a girl. He had his toy pistol and he'd thought that would make a girl frightened enough to go with him.

He'd found himself a prime lookout point, watched women crossing the street far below his perch in the parking lot, and finally chose the one he wanted—a slender woman with long red-gold hair and very full breasts. She wore a bright red linen dress, the hemline stopping at mid thigh, and tantalizing high-heeled pumps.

He didn't know it, nor would it have mattered to him, but her name was Sharon Wood and she was twenty-four years old. She was, on that gloriously warm April day, a perfect target for Jerry Brudos. Actually a gutsy, intelligent young woman, Sharon was having a bad day on April 21. The last thing on her mind was caution. She had far too many other things to worry about. Her abduction should have gone smoothly.

Jerry Brudos, like the majority of serial killers, could pick up on that temporary vulnerability almost as a wolf catches the scent of fear in his prey. The distracted victim is the ideal victim for a predator.

It was three-thirty that afternoon when Sharon left the Portland State history department where she worked as a secretary. She had been married for seven years, had two little children, and her marriage was about to blow all to smithereens. On this afternoon, her about-to-be-ex-husband had agreed to meet with her, and her mind was on that meeting.

She was feeling lousy physically, too, suffering with a middle-ear infection and using antibiotics; her hearing, at best, was not acute. Now sounds came to her muffled and indistinct. She was near-sighted, and adjusting to newly prescribed contact lenses. The senses she needed most were blurred that afternoon.

It wasn't surprising that Sharon was distracted and depressed. She couldn't even find her damned car keys, and she'd had to dump out the contents of her purse on her desk before she left her office. She hoped she could find the extra key she'd hidden in a magnetic box under the car frame.

Sharon tapped her foot impatiently as she waited for the "Walk" sign to flash at the corner of Broadway and Harrison in downtown Portland. She hadn't the vaguest awareness of the big man watching her from his perch high up in the parking garage across the street. Eight stories high with open sides, packed with cars belonging to some of the 9,000 Portland State students and faculty, the parking garage had always seemed safe enough to Sharon.

And it *was* broad daylight. People streamed by her on either side as she waited.

As Sharon Wood headed across the street, she hoped that she could find the spare key, and then she realized she wasn't even sure on which level she'd parked that morning. She was going to be late meeting her estranged husband.

Sharon would recall years later that she had never before in her life encountered any manner of sexual violence. . . .

"As I sped down the steps into the basement level, my high heels clicked on the concrete," she recalled. "The heavy doors shut automatically behind me, cutting me off from daylight and the campus population. I walked about fifteen feet forward and looked around for my car, and realized I was on the wrong level."

Sharon turned to go back up the dead-space area between the parking levels, and sensed—if only obliquely—that someone was behind her. She recalls it was only an awareness of someone in back of her, not a distinct impression of a man or a woman.

"Instinct told me not to return to the more isolated stair area, so I pivoted and started for the daylight entrance on the far side of the building," she said.

Sharon still had not looked around, but she walked rapidly, giving into that "gut feeling" that warns of nameless, faceless danger. But she had walked only a few steps when she felt a light tap on her shoulder.

She turned her head and looked directly into Jerry Brudos' pale blue eyes.

"I could sense the evil and I *knew* I was going to die. . . ."

And then she saw the pistol. The big, freckled man promised her, "If you don't scream, I won't shoot you."

Almost unconsciously, Sharon Wood made a choice. "No!" she screamed at the top of her lungs, at the same time backing away from the man with the gun. Undeterred, Jerry Brudos stepped quickly behind her again and grabbed her in an arm-lock around her neck. She was five feet four inches tall, and weighed 118 pounds. The man who held her in a "half nelson" was over six feet tall and weighed 210 pounds.

Kicking and screaming, Sharon continued to shout "No!" She tried to grab for the gun that was right in front of her face, twisting and pulling at the fat fingers that held it.

The man's huge hand passed close to her mouth, and she bit into the fleshy thickness of his thumb as hard as she could. She tasted blood, *his* blood, and she tried to let go. But, in her terror, her jaw had locked. She *could* not release his hand, and they danced a kind of crazy dance in the dimness of the parking garage as Jerry Brudos tried to free himself of the kicking, biting blonde who had seemed such an easy target.

In desperation, he wound his free hand around and around in Sharon Wood's long strawberry blonde hair and pulled her head toward the concrete, forcing her body to the ground.

"Oh, God," she thought. "Now, he's going to rape me right here."

Brudos still had a grip on Sharon's hair, and began to beat her head against the floor. Hazily, she saw a Volkswagen "Bug" driving toward them as she began to lose consciousness. Only then did her jaw relax from its muscle spasm and her attacker pull his thumb free. Through bleared eyes she saw him pick up his gun and run. How odd, she thought hazily: Once *he* became the captive, he acted scared to death . . . he was fighting to get away from *me*.

And then she passed out.

Portland police patrolmen arrived at the parking garage to take Sharon Wood's statement about the crime, which was listed as "aggravated assault." Tragically, no connection was made at the time between the attack on Sharon in Portland and the dead girls found floating in the river near Corvallis.

Of the two officers responding, one told Sharon, "Don't you think you took a hell of a chance—fighting a man with a gun?" His partner disagreed, "I think you did the right thing."

In this instance, of course, she had. She would not know for years the details of her attacker's other crime. Sharon Wood was left with a pounding headache, wrenched muscles, scrapes, bruises, torn clothing, and nightmares.

But she was alive.

She was one of Jerry Brudos few failures.

He'd had to get out of there quickly. He had kept his head, though. If he'd run, somebody would have been suspicious. He'd forced himself to walk away casually—fast, but casually. He climbed the ramp to the next floor and walked to his car. Nobody stopped him. But his thumb throbbed for the rest of the day.

It was humiliating to have something like that happen, and he'd still been so full of the urge for a woman. He'd tried again the next day, right in Salem. That girl was a young one, not more than fourteen or fifteen, and he'd thought he was lucky to find a schoolgirl out of school at ten-thirty in the morning on a Tuesday. She was just hurrying along the Southern Pacific Railroad tracks headed for Parrish Junior High when he spotted her.

He'd tried to act like it was urgent when he said, "I want you to come with me. I won't hurt you," and then he'd grabbed at her coat at the shoulder and pulled her between two houses, and showed her the gun.

She'd been scared, all right, and he'd told her, "I won't rape you. I wouldn't do that."

"Let go of me," she'd said, as if she wasn't afraid of him at all.

Then he'd led her toward the borrowed sports car and told her to get in, and the little bitch had broken away from him and run screaming for help to a woman who was working in her yard.

He'd had to run too, get in his car, and gun the motor before somebody got a glimpse of the license plate.

Two failures had hurt his ego some, and made him determined that he'd be successful the next day.

He smiled. He had been perfectly successful. He'd walked right into the parking garage at Lloyd Center and found the pretty girl in the beige coat. He'd caught her before she could get into her red Volkswagen and he'd held out the little tin police badge—and she'd fallen for it.

And now he was okay again. The secret was to learn from his failures, not to dwell on them.

There were so many girls around. Even though the police had found the two he'd left in the river, he didn't worry that anybody was close to him; they had no idea who he was. He thought about all the girls there were on college campuses—more than any other place. They were all young, and most of them were pretty.

He developed a new plan. It worked beautifully. All he had to do was call one of the dorms and ask for a common name—"Susan" or "Lisa" or "Mary." Somebody always came to the phone, and he pretended that a friend had given him her name. Some of them wanted to know *which* friend and hung up on him when he couldn't come up with a name. But he managed to get three dates that way. He took them out for coffee and talked with them. None of them were exactly his type, but he enjoyed bringing up the newspaper articles about the dead girls in the river, and it turned him on to see how nervous it made them. Talk about jumpy! When he reached out to touch them on the shoulder, they practically leaped out of their skin.

Seeing them afraid and nervous was so stimulating that he'd been driven to steal more underwear for his collection. He had an improvement on his "panty raids," too; he wore women's underwear when he crept through the dorms, and a pair of large-sized women's pedal pushers. It made his forays more exciting when he dressed that way.

He had no doubt that his "blind" telephone calls would soon win him a coffee date with a girl who *was* his type. When he found the next one, he would take her with him. . . .

— 12 —

Jim Stovall, Jerry Frazier, and Gene Daugherty were living and breathing the cases of Karen Sprinker and Linda Salee. They did not delude themselves into thinking that the girls' deaths were the final acts of a pattern. They knew it would continue if the killer wasn't caught, and it made everything else in their lives take a back seat.

During the day, Stovall and Frazier plodded through junkyards in Salem and Portland with Lieutenant Daugherty, trying to get a line on the origin of the auto parts used to weight the girls' bodies. The parts had come from a Chevrolet, a model produced between 1953 and 1962. The engine head had weighed sixty pounds. The task of tracing the parts to one particular car from the hundreds of thousands that came off assembly lines in a nine-year period was almost hopeless. There were no serial numbers to compare, no way at all to follow the history of the junked vehicle back to Detroit and then through a series of owners. But there was the faintest of possibilities that some junkyard owner would remember selling the parts. And there was more likelihood that the auto parts could be traced than that the origin of the mass-produced mechanic's cloths could. The nylon cord and the copper wire used to fasten the engine parts to the bodies was also mass-produced, available from uncountable sources. The black bra was old, purchased years before, and had been sold through outlets all over America.

It was quite possible that there were more than one killer or that the murderer had had an accomplice. It would have taken a man of Herculean strength to lift both the bodies and the heavy auto parts and carry them to the riverbank. No average man could have done it.

Where the man actually lived was another puzzle to be worked out. Linda Slawson and Linda Salee had disappeared from Portland's city limits, and Detective James Cunningham of the Portland police was assigned to those cases, but Linda Salee had been found in Benton County and Linda Slawson had never been found at all. Karen Sprinker had been reported missing from Salem and had been found in Benton County. Jan Whitney's case was being investigated by the Oregon State Police, and only God knew where her body was.

Stovall and Frazier traveled continually, accompanied by Daugherty, checking in with police departments in the Willamette Valley to be sure they weren't missing any clues, information that, taken alone, meant nohing, but when added to the growing file of facts and leads, might mean everything.

Stovall typed the missing and dead girls' names on a small file card and tacked them up over his desk. He was looking for a common denominator. "What kind of spook are we looking for?" he asked himself again and again.

Since he had no face, and no name, and precious little physical evidence to help him find the killer, he tried a technique that had worked for him before. He drew on his background in criminal psychology, on the few facts he knew for certain, and on the "gut feelings" that every superior detective hooks onto when there is nothing else to do.

Stovall placed a clean sheet of paper on his desk and picked up the felt pen he always favors. In his distinctive printing, he wrote a question mark, and then began to fill the page with the thoughts that came tumbling into his head.

? Killer is . . .
1. Between twenty and thirty—because all victims are young.

2. Of at least average intelligence—knots used to tie parts to bodies skilled.

3. An electrician—copper wire on the bodies wound one turn around and broken, then wound twice as electricians do—twisted in fashion common to electrical wiring.

4. Probably from broken home—with one parent gone . . . or the child of a strong mother and weak father . . . strong dislike for mother shown by desecration of female bodies. HATES WOMEN.

5. Probable record of antisocial behavior going far back.

6. Not participant in contact sports—women strangled but not beaten. Strangulation required little force.

7. Not a steady worker. No reason, beyond girls' disappearances at odd hours of day.

8. Driven by a cycle of some sort—possible pseudo-menstrual? All girls vanished toward end of month:
   Slawson: January 26
   Whitney: November 26
   Sprinker: March 27
   Salee: April 23

Even with his training and experience taken into account, it is eerie to see just how close Stovall came to visualizing the man he sought. He could not actually *know* these things at the time, for his list, although based on the few facts known, was almost entirely the creation of a subliminal awareness—as if the detective had, indeed, locked into the murderer's mind.

Stovall searched in May 1969 for his "common denominator"—some way to tie a specific suspect to the pattern of deaths.

He assumed that the killer had to be someone familiar with the area from Corvallis to Portland. His origins or recent living arrangements had to have been centered at one time around the Long Tom River. It was too isolated a waterway for someone to have stumbled on it accidentally. Undoubtedly the bodies had been left in the river during nighttime hours by someone who could literally find his way to its banks in the dark. A stranger would have fallen in himself with one misstep.

The man had to be very, very strong. Stovall felt that it was only one man. Incidents of serial murder—lust murder—rarely involve more than one killer; that kind of killing results from a solitary aberration, a secret compulsion that the killer cannot, will not, share with anyone else. No, he was looking for a large man, because a small man could not have carried the bodies and their heavy weights.

The killer undoubtedly looked normal—as most sexual criminals do. The maniacal rapist, frothing at the mouth, is a fiction writer's killer. Most actual rapists are average-looking—even attractive—and usually have some manner of relationship with a woman. They rape and kill because of an inner rage, because they are driven compulsively to do so. If the killer's black side was obvious, Stovall doubted that he would have been able to get close enough to the victims to abduct them.

Jim Stovall studied a map of Oregon. Since the killer had roved from possibly as far south as Eugene and as far north as Portland, his residence was probably somewhere in between the two cities, a "safe house" to run to when the heat was on after each disappearance. The most likely city for the killer's home base would be Corvallis or Salem.

Karen Sprinker had spent most of her time in Corvallis while she attended Oregon State University; she was seized in Salem. Was there a connection? Was it possible that she had known her killer . . . or that he might have watched her for some time, and stalked her to Salem?

Daughtery and Stovall agreed that the obvious place to begin intensive questioning was Callahan Hall, where Karen Sprinker had lived. There were hundreds of coeds rooming in Callahan and in other dorms on the Corvallis campus.

Gene Daugherty packed up and moved to Corvallis to organize a massive interviewing program. He would literally live there until a break came—if it did. Daugherty found the Corvallis Police Department and the college authorities magnificently cooperative. The police department provided two detectives, B. J. Miller and "Frenchie" De Lamere, who joined in the search for the killer. The interview teams would work each day and every evening, talking to coeds at fifteen-minute intervals.

"First, we talked with all the girls who had known Karen even slightly. We asked them about her dates, and then we asked them about their own dates. How many dates did they have, and who were they with? Had any of them received peculiar phone calls? Had they been taken to strange places? Had they been in contact with any strange or unusual people? Anything that might have been out of the ordinary—no matter how unimportant it might have seemed. Then we talked to the girls who had not known Karen, and asked them the same questions."

The girls interviewed were subdued, sometimes frightened when they talked of Karen. It could have happened to any of them, and they knew it. Yes, most of them had dated frequently, and it seemed okay to date men they had met on campus. A campus atmosphere seemed safer somehow; it wasn't as thought you were dating strangers you'd met in a city.

Now all of the women interviewed tried to remember anything that had happened to them that had seemed a little off-center. Some of them were embarrassed, but most of them were quite frank in their eagerness to help. Not surprisingly, many of them had had dates with college boys who were sexually aggressive—but not peculiar about it, and none of them had used force.

After interviewing dozens of girls and filling countless yellow legal pads with notes, Daugherty and the interview teams began to get a little discouraged. It was such a long shot, really, to hope that one of the coeds was going to give the killer to them. Perhaps there *was* no good information to be gleaned at Oregon State.

But asking questions is a major part of a detective's work. A million answers may be utterly useless, and a thousand possible witnesses have to be dismissed with a "thank you for your time." But the right answer cannot be jarred free unless a concerted effort is made. When that one answer shines through, it is worth all the tedium.

And so the detectives worked each day in the stuffy little room off the main lounge of Callahan Hall. Outside, students threw Frisbees on the green, and the lilacs grew in thick clusters, their blooms filling the air with fragrance. Occasionally, laughter carried through the open window, making the grim investigation seem incongruous. And also reminding the detectives that Karen Sprinker could never again return to this campus.

With each new girl, the same questions. "Who have you dated in the last three months?"

And mostly, the same answers. Boys from the dorm next door, boys they'd known in their hometowns. There were a few oddballs in the bunch. One girl had dated a man who wanted to do nothing but have her sit quietly while he played his flute—"very badly"—for her. "I turned him down the next time he called."

There were a couple of girls who'd dated a fellow who wanted to go to Portland and seek out porno movies. "He was kind of weird—but not that weird," one said. "He didn't try anything."

Despite the girls' evaluations of the men they mentioned as harmless, detectives checked out all the ones who had been in any way peculiar, and they all cleared.

And then three or four young women mentioned receiving phone calls from a stranger. He had asked for them by their first name, but none of them had ever met the man before. One girl tried to remember what he had talked about. "Let's see . . . it was a couple of weeks ago. This guy said that he'd been a prisoner in Vietnam for three years. Then he started in on this garbage about how he possessed extraordinary powers in ESP—that kind of thing. Like he was supposed to be clairvoyant or something. He wanted me to meet him for a Coke, but I said no."

"Did he give you a name?" Daugherty asked.

"No . . ." The girl shook her head slowly. "Or if he did, I can't remember. I just wasn't interested. I mean,

I didn't know him, and his conversation was a little odd."

After hearing about the same "Vietnam vet" from three more girls, Daugherty began to grow a little more enthusiastic about the lead. He was fascinated by the story told by a girl the next day. She too had received an unsolicited phone call from a man who said he was a Vietnam veteran. But, most interesting of all, *she* had agreed to meet the caller in the lounge of her dorm!

"He wasn't offensive when he called; he didn't say anything suggestive or raunchy," she explained. "He said he was really lonesome because he'd been away in the war for years, and he just wanted to meet a girl who would have a cup of coffee with him and talk. When I mentioned I was taking some psychology courses, he said that he'd been a patient at Walter Reed Hospital. He said he had learned a whole new method of study there and that I might be interested in hearing about it. I guess it was kind of foolish to make a date, but I felt a little sorry for him."

"So he did come over to your dorm?"

"Yes. He came over." She laughed nervously. "He turned out about like most blind dates do. He was a lot older than I expected—about thirty. He wasn't very good-looking. Kind of tubby, and he was losing his hair. I mean, he wasn't exactly a knight on a white horse or anything."

"What did you talk about?"

"At first we stayed in the lounge and just talked about general things—the weather, and studying, although he never did tell me about whatever that special method of study was. Just dumb stuff, the way you do when you don't really know a person. Oh, there was something . . ."

Daugherty looked up sharply. "What?"

"Well, he put his hand on my shoulder and began to massage it . . . and then he said—I don't know how to explain it—he said, 'Be sad.' "

" 'Be *sad*'?"

"Yes. Wasn't that peculiar? He wanted me to be sad or look sad or something, and I laughed and said I didn't feel sad about anything. Then he said, 'Think of those two girls they found in the river. Those girls who got killed. That was an awful thing that happened to them.' "

"That must have frightened you a little."

"No, not really. Everybody on campus had been talking about it, because it was in all the papers and because one of the girls was a student here. But I guess I just wasn't thinking too much about it. He asked me if I would go out with him and get a Coke, and I did."

"He didn't say or do anything else that seemed odd?"

"Well, kind of," the girl told Daugherty and Jerry Frazier and B. J. Miller, who had moved closer to listen to this most interesting incident. "He was telling me all about self-defense. He said most girls think that they should kick a man in the groin, but that's wrong. He said you might miss and make the guy mad and you'd be off balance. He said you should kick him in the shins first, and then in the groin."

"Anything else?"

"Well, I told him that I had heard it would take at least two men to carry an auto part and a body down to the river bank, and he said he agreed with me—but when he was leaving, it was kind of creepy, what he said. . . ."

"What was that?" Miller asked.

"He said, 'Why did you change your mind and come with me?' And I said I guessed I was curious. And he said, 'How did you know I would bring you back home and not take you to the river and strangle you?' Wasn't that kind of weird?"

That gave the detectives pause. Frazier cleared his throat and asked the girl about her blind date's car.

"Oh, he had an old junker of a car, and it was dirty and there were kids' clothes in it. I thought he might have been married, but he didn't mention that he was. He did say something about having had to replace the motor in his car recently."

"Can you describe the car?"

"Not really. I'm really bad on cars. It was so dirty,

and it was night, so I can't even tell you the color. It was a station wagon, and I think it had Oregon plates."

"Tell me again what he looked like. Describe him as if I had to pick him out from a crowd of people on the street."

"Okay. He was tall, close to six feet. And heavy. Not fat . . . but soft around the middle. His hair was blondish-red, and like I said, it was thinning on top—he kind of combed it forward. Let me see . . . His eyes slanted down at the corners. Bad dresser. Oh, and his complexion was pale and he had freckles."

"That's very good," Daugherty complimented her. "That helps. Have you seen him again?"

She shook her head. "He said he would be back in two days, but he never called. I didn't really care. A lot of guys will say they're going to call you. It's just something to say, and I wasn't interested in him anyway."

"I want you to do something for me, if you will," Daugherty said. "If he calls again, tell him you'll see him."

"Oh . . ." The young woman looked alarmed. "I . . ."

"No, you won't have to meet him alone. Make a date, but give him some excuse why you can't see him right away. Then call this number." He handed her a card with the number of the Corvallis police on it. "They'll be alerted. They'll be here before he gets here. Under no circumstances go anyplace with him. Say you'll meet him in the lounge. Okay?"

"Okay. But he might never call again. I think he could tell I wasn't that crazy about him."

"Maybe he will. Maybe he won't. Just be sure you delay him if he does, and call the police."

Freckles. That part of the description rang a bell in Jim Stovall's carefully compartmentalized brain when he heard the coed's description. There weren't that many men who had freckles, especially in the spring before the sunburn season. Salem detectives had been going through all complaints that had come into their department since the first of the year, looking for something that might resemble the Karen Sprinker

case. Among other incidents, they had pulled the
attempted-kidnaping complaint made by fifteen-year-
old Liane Brumley. Stovall had reread it, and now he
remembered "freckles." He checked the file. Liane
Brumley had been terribly frightened by the man who
loomed up in front of her as she hurried along the
railroad tracks, saved, possibly, by her decision to
scream and run for help.

April 22. Ten-thirty A.M. That was only one day
before Linda Salee had disappeared from Lloyd Center in Portland. The suspect had said, "I won't rape
you. I wouldn't do that." Stovall figured the man was
protesting too much: with a gun and his orders to the
Brumley girl to get into his car, what *had* he planned
to do with her? Neither Linda Salee nor Karen Sprinker
had been shot, but a gun would have been a strong
convincer to force a girl to go with the killer without
screaming. Stovall was grateful that Liane Brumley
had screamed; it could well have saved her life.

He ran his finger under the physical description.
"Tall, over six feet." That difference was negligible—
witnesses are off on height estimation more than any
other factor in identification. "Sandy hair. *Freckles.*"

For a moment, he felt exhilaration. Was it possible
that all the days spent interviewing and going through
car graveyards and driving between one police department and another—all those hundreds of man-hours
worked by himself and dozens of others—would come
down to something as simple as freckles?

There they were. Two incidents. Both in Salem—
but with a connection, however tenuous, in Corvallis
now.

Could this really be a break, or was it only wishful
thinking?

— 13 —

It was nearing the end of the third full week in May, a time bracket that made Jim Stovall and Gene Daugherty nervous. If the killer operated under the stress of a pseudo-menstrual cycle as Stovall suspected, his prowling time had rolled around again. Somewhere—in Salem, or Corvallis, or Portland, or maybe some other city in Oregon—the killer would be getting restless. He had taken Karen on March 27, Linda on April 23. His compulsion to stalk and seize a woman might well be at fever pitch, and there was no way in hell they could warn every pretty young woman in the state to be on guard.

It was possible that the discovery of the bodies in the Long Tom and the resultant publicity had made the faceless man cautious—but they doubted it. On the contrary, all the press coverage might have honed his appetite, appealed to some need for fame—or, in his case, infamy. He might feel that a gauntlet had been flung down. He might just want to prove that he was smarter than the cops.

It was Sunday night, May 25. In Callahan Hall, the young woman who had promised to call the police if she ever heard from her scruffy admirer again sat in her room studying. She was a little tense, but not much; it had been eleven days since she'd had her Coke date with a stranger, and she hadn't heard anything more from him.

And then the buzzer next to her door blurted its steady tone, and she jumped. She moved quickly to press down on it to show that she had heard and would go down the hall to the phone. On her way, she told herself it could be anyone—her mother, or a girlfriend, or one of the men she dated casually.

But when she picked up the phone, she recognized the slightly hesitant voice of the big freckled man. And she fought to keep her voice calm.

"How about a Coke and some conversation?"

"I . . . I thought I wouldn't hear from you again. This is kind of short notice."

"Sorry. I've been busy. But I could be over there in, say, fifteen minutes."

"Oh . . ." she delayed, "I'd like to see you, but I can't go anywhere until I wash my hair. It's a mess."

"That doesn't matter."

"Well, it does to me. I could be ready in about forty-five minutes—maybe an hour. If that's okay, why don't I meet you downstairs then?"

She held her breath while he argued that she didn't have to bother getting fixed up, and then she heard him agree to the delay.

As soon as she heard the line go dead, she dialed the Corvallis Police Department. "He called. I managed to stall him by telling him I have to wash my hair. He'll be downstairs in the lounge in about forty-five minutes."

"We'll be there. We'll be waiting when he walks in."

B. J. Miller and Frenchie De Lamere, in plain clothes, sat in the lounge out of the line of vision of anyone coming in the door. They waited. Ten minutes. Twenty minutes. Several young men came in, obviously college boys waiting to pick up dates. Ten more minutes. And then they saw him, a big, hulking man who seemed out of place. He wore a T-shirt and wrinkled "high-water" slacks, topped by a Pendleton jacket of a somewhat garish plaid. He was no kid. He had to be thirty, maybe older. The big man looked around the lounge, failed to see his date, and sat on a couch where he could watch the stairs.

De Lamere and Miller moved over to him and showed their badges. He looked up, hardly startled, and smiled slightly.

"We'd like to ask you a few questions, sir—if you don't mind."

"No, not at all. What can I do for you?"

"We'd like to have your name."

"It's Brudos. Jerry Brudos."

"You live here in Corvallis?"

He shook his head. "No. I live in Salem. I used to live here, but I just came over to mow a friend's lawn and check out his place. He's on vacation."

The answers came quite smoothly, and neither officer could detect any signs of stress in Brudos. No perspiration. No fidgeting. He gave his Center Street address. He said that he was an electrician by trade, and admitted a little sheepishly that he was married and had two young children. He gave the name and address of the friend's property where he'd been working.

There was no legal reason to arrest Jerry Brudos or even to hold him for questioning. The officers thanked him, and he left the lounge. They noted that he drove a beat-up greenish-blue station wagon that was *not* a General Motors product. They jotted down the license number and returned to headquarters to begin a check that might verify what Brudos had told them.

Jerry Brudos' story of doing yardwork for a friend was verified. He did know the occupant of the house whose address he'd given, and the man was on vacation. Neighbors said Brudos often worked there, and had during the daylight hours of Sunday, May 25.

On the surface, he seemed to pass muster.

But that was only on the surface. Jerry Brudos' name was in the hopper and the investigative process had begun. Jim Stovall and Gene Daugherty received the information gleaned by the Corvallis officers, and used it as the bare bones of a dossier on the man— Jerome Henry Brudos.

Brudos' record of commitment to the Oregon State Hospital indicated that he had shown evidence of sexual violence as far back as his teens. There were, however, no recent records of treatment. Either he had gotten well or he had managed to avoid treatment.

He had no arrest record as an adult. That might

mean they were focusing on the wrong man—or it might only mean he was clever.

As Stovall and Daugherty worked rapidly to back-track on Brudos, they found too many "coincidences" to be explained away. In January, 1968 Jerry Brudos had lived in the same neighborhood worked by the young encyclopedia salesgirl—the missing Linda Slawson. Brudos had indicated that he'd moved to Salem in August or September 1968 and gone to work in Lebanon, Oregon—hard by the I-5 freeway where Jan Whitney had vanished in November. His current job was in Halsey—only six miles from the body sites in the Long Tom. And, of course, when Karen Sprinker disappeared from Meier and Frank on March 27, Brudos had lived only blocks away. . . .

And he was an electrician.

The investigative team in Salem was anxious to get a look at this Jerry Brudos. Jerry Frazier made the first contact, a casual conversation outside the little house on Center Street. Frazier and Jerry Brudos talked in in the old garage Jerry used for his shop and darkroom. The detective was fascinated with the place, and made a note to tell Stovall about the profusion of ropes, knots, the hook in the ceiling. He couldn't say just why the paraphernalia made the hairs on the back of his neck stand up—but it did.

Jerry Brudos talked obscurely about "problems"—that some problems didn't need to be cured, that some made him feel that he was dipping his hand in a cookie jar and how "You're afraid of getting caught."

But when Frazier pressed him about "problems," Brudos just said he had jobs where he couldn't get along with his fellow workers—that he lived in a world full of people but he was always alone.

When he returned to Salem police headquarters and reported to Stovall, he said, "It looks good. He seems calm enough about being contacted, but I'd like for you and Ginther to go back with me and see what you think."

"Any special reason?" Stovall asked.

"Just a feeling. . . ."

Stovall, Frazier, and Greg Ginther, another member

of the team, drove out to Center Street to talk again with Jerry Brudos. Until now, Stovall had had no image to focus on, nothing more than the Corvallis coed's description of her suitor and a black-and-white picture in the files.

The man they saw did not look overtly dangerous; he looked, instead, somewhat like an overgrown Pillsbury Doughboy. They had expected a huge muscular man, and this man betrayed no evidence of exceptional strength. His lidded eyes sloped at the outer corners and his chin and cheeks were blurred with flesh.

He looked like a loser. The kind of guy who sits at the end of the bar nursing his beer, always a little bloated, with no confidence to start up a conversation. He had to have been the sort of kid who got picked last in sandlot ball. He was clearly no ladies' man, at least not in the accepted sense of the term.

Stovall studied Brudos' speech patterns, his mannerisms, the way he moved and walked. He intended to show Liane Brumley the picture he had of Brudos, and he wanted to be able to "listen" to her recollections of her near-abduction with a solid memory of the man who was Jerry Brudos.

He saw Brudos' old station wagon parked nearby; that didn't seem to match Liane's description of the vehicle her would-be kidnapper had driven. She had said it was a small sports car.

"This your only car?" Stovall asked.

"Yeah."

"You ever drive anything else?"

"My friend's sometimes—it's a Karmann Ghia."

That fit closer. Stovall let it pass without comment.

The investigators asked if they could have another look around the garage. It looked like anybody's garage, divided by some plywood into smaller rooms, except that Frazier and Stovall noted the weights were still hanging from rope there. There was something about the knots that looked familiar—instantly reminiscent of the knots that had bound the auto parts to the dead girls' bodies. The rope was a quarter-inch, and there was some nylon cord that looked to be about three-sixteenths of an inch. Both the right size, the right material.

Brudos half-smiled as he said to Frazier, "You seem to be interested in that knot. Go ahead and take it if you want to."

Frazier moved quickly, cutting two short lengths, and being sure to include the distinctive knot. The rope and cord was common enough stuff; the lab could only give a "very probable" on something so widely distributed—but the knot was special.

Brudos did not ask if they would be back; he re-remained quite calm.

If the probe into the girls' murders and disappearances had seemed to lag before, now it accelerated to a frenzied pace. Stovall obtained the old black-and-white photo of Jerry Brudos and included it in a "lay-down"—a montage of mug shots. He took that lay-down to Liane Brumley and asked her if she recognized any of the men. She studied the photos carefully and then tapped the picture of Jerry Brudos.

"That looks like him—but the man who grabbed me had freckles. This man doesn't."

But he did. They just didn't show up in the photograph.

In fiction, it would be enough—all the pieces falling cleverly into place. In truth, it was only a beginning. To arrest a man, and then to take him before a jury, the state has to be armed with physical evidence—something twelve of his peers can see and touch and feel, or something a criminalist can tell them he has seen under a scanning electron microscope. The old axiom that a criminal always leaves something of himself at the scenes of his crimes, and always takes something of the scene away with him—no matter how minute—is truer than it ever was.

That was what Stovall and Daugherty and Frazier and the rest of the team had to find. What they knew now was that circumstantial evidence was piling up, that probably Jerome Brudos *had* been the man who tried to abduct Liane Brumley. The rest they only suspected. They needed all the bits and pieces of physical evidence that waited—somewhere—to be found. Something they could slip into plastic bags with their own initials added, something they could haul into a courtroom when the time was right.

Despite his placid exterior, Jerry Brudos had begun to feel a little uneasy. He sensed he was being tailed by the police. They hadn't gotten into his workshop, had only glanced at the locked door beyond the garage, but he figured they might come back. As far as he knew, there was nothing in there that would do them any good anyway, but the thought of them pussyfooting around his shop and darkroom was unsettling. Worse, he could not bear to have his movements hampered—and the police were hampering him by following him wherever he went.

He called Salem attorney Dale Drake and asked for an appointment the following day—May 27. When he faced Drake in his office, Jerry Brudos said, "I'm having some problems with the police. I'd like you to investigate and find out. I'll pay you for checking into it."

Drake refused the retainer, telling Brudos not to worry about money for the moment. He would stand by to represent him if, indeed, Brudos did have "police trouble."

The police were having a bit of trouble of their own, or, rather, were walking a very delicate path to be sure that they did not blow a case that was not yet fully formed. They did not yet have their damning physical evidence. They could not arrest Brudos for murder and hope to win a conviction. They wanted no pegs a defense team could hang their hats on. Rather, they wanted to give Brudos enough rope to hang himself, and that meant it was prudent to let him stay free where they could watch his movements. But there was danger there; if he should panic and bolt, they might lose him. They had an ace in the hole: the Liane Brumley case. If an arrest seemed essential, they could get a warrant on that case.

And so, when Brudos pulled out to head down the I-5 freeway to his job in Halsey south of Corvallis, a sneaker car was behind him. When he returned home, he was followed. For the next few days there was not a moment when Jerry Brudos was free of surveillance—subtle, but always there.

Beyond the fear that he might cut and run, there was the possibility that he might harm still another girl; the dangerous time period between the twenty-second and the end of the month was only at the halfway point. If they had the right man, and if they let him slip away from their observation, more tragedy might result.

But Jerry Brudos appeared to be following ordinary everyday patterns. He went to work. He came home, and he seemed to stay home in the evenings. On occasion, the family car pulled out and they saw that it was driven by a small dark-haired woman—Brudos' wife. She seemed unaware that something cataclysmic was happening in her world.

On Wednesday, May 28, at ten minutes to eight, a search warrant was served on the two vehicles available to Jerry Brudos. Brudos signed a Miranda Rights Card with a bland expression on his face. If he was getting more and more nervous, he didn't show it. His green station wagon proved to be spotless. It had been thoroughly washed both inside and out. In fact, it was *damp* inside.

Brudos smiled and said, "I took it through a fifty-cent car wash, and my little boy accidentally rolled down a window."

Jerry Frazier found Jerry Brudos almost too calm.

Later, Brudos would confide in Frazier, "I don't think you got anything out of the car. There's something, but I can't put my finger on it. There is kind of a link missing, having to do with the car. But I wasn't worried about it. I just felt like I wasn't involved. There was no doubt in my mind, until you compared the ropes. If I knew you were going to do that, I would have gotten rid of the rope." (But would he? Hadn't he so much as *offered* the knot to Jerry Frazier, almost begged him to take it into evidence?)

Stovall, Frazier, Greg Ginther, and Lieutenants "Manny" Boyes and Robert Pinnick of the Oregon

State Police Crime Lab searched and processed the 1964 Karmann Ghia, too, and took away almost infinitesimal fragments of evidence.

During the long evening, Jerry Brudos called his attorney three times, but let the searchers continue.

On Friday evening, May 30, 1969, Jim Stovall and Gene Daugherty left Salem for Corvallis, armed with a Marion County District Court Arrest Warrant charging Jerry Brudos with Assault While Armed with a Dangerous Weapon (in the Liane Brumley case). It was 5:05 p.m.

Before they could reach their destination, the stakeout team radioed that the Brudos family had left Corvallis, and was heading north on the I-5 freeway. Jerry Brudos was behind the wheel of the 1963 green Comet station wagon, Oregon License 7P–5777, when they left Corvallis, but enroute they changed drivers, and Darcie took the wheel while Jerry lay in the back seat. But they weren't headed home; Darcie drove right through Salem, and continued north toward Portland.

The waiting was over. Daugherty and Stovall could not risk letting Jerry Brudos escape into the metropolitan area of Portland—or perhaps even farther north into Washington State and then 250 miles to the Canadian border. The two detectives fell in behind the state police "sneaker" cars trailing the green station wagon.

There could be no more holding back and watching. The first car behind the Brudos vehicle pulled nearer and the trooper flicked on the revolving red light. Darcie Brudos saw it and eased into the slow lane, coming to a stop on the shoulder.

It was 7:28 p.m. Daugherty approached from one side, and Stovall and B. J. Miller from the other. They saw the worried-looking woman behind the wheel, the little boy and girl in the front seat. Darcie Brudos reached for her driver's license and started to ask what she had done wrong. Daugherty shook his head slightly and shone his flashlight into the back seat.

Jerry Brudos was there, hidden under a blanket.

"You're under arrest. Get out of the car, please."

With Brudos blinking his eyes in the glare of the phalanx of state police cars, Daugherty read him his rights from a Miranda card.

And then Daugherty and Stovall transported Jerry Brudos to the Salem City Police Station where he was booked, photographed, and committed to jail.

Stovall snapped a picture of the big man in the plaid shirt with his own Leica, catching the image of the man they'd searched for so long. Here, he believed, was the face of the man that fit the list he'd made.

But as Brudos stripped to change into jail coveralls, his clothing no longer resembled a typical Oregon working man's. Jerry Brudos was wearing women's sheer panties. He looked up to see Stovall and Daugherty exchange glances.

Brudos reddened, and explained, "I have sensitive skin."

The detectives said nothing.

Jerry Frazier searched Jerry Brudos' wallet as the prisoner was booked. Tucked deep in one of the leather folds, he found a tiny photograph of a nude woman, a rectangle measuring one inch by one and a half inches. It looked as though it was a Polaroid that had been trimmed from its original size. The head and feet were missing. Frazier could just make out a Sears Craftsman tool chest behind the girl. He placed it in a glassine envelope and put a property tag on it: #2017.

Who was the girl in the picture? Frazier wondered if she was still alive—whoever she was.

Darcie Brudos' nightmare had begun; she had no idea what was happening. She had watched as her husband was handcuffed and placed in the back seat of a police car. She had quieted her sobbing children, and then she had turned around and followed the police caravan back to Salem.

Darcie waited while her husband was booked into jail. When she finally had a moment to talk to him, she begged, "Jerry, what is it?"

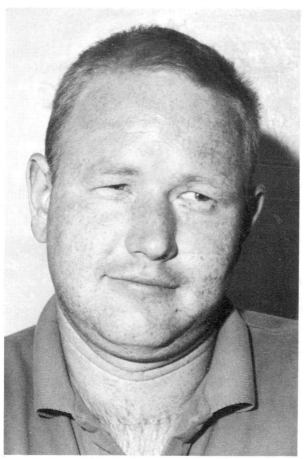
Jerome Brudos, the "Lust Killer,"
as he was being arrested
(photographed by Detective Jim Stovall).

Karen Sprinker, a 19-year-old freshman at Oregon State University at Corvallis, was kidnapped from a Salem, Oregon, department store.

Linda Salee, a petite, athletic 22-year-old, was kidnapped in Portland, Oregon.

Sharon Wood, a 24-year-old secretary, was attacked by Brudos in the parking garage at Portland State University. She fought him and escaped, battered but alive.

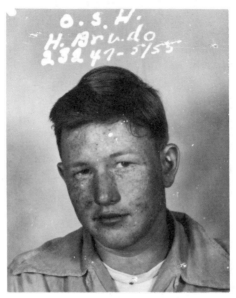

Jerry Brudos at 17. His attack on two teenage girls led him to be committed to the Oregon State Hospital for the treatment of sexual deviation and fetishism.

Detective Jim Stovall of the Salem, Oregon, police department discovered the shocking details of the Brudos murders.

Detective Jerry Frazier, standing, and Jim Stovall, seated, search Brudos' house after his confession. Frazier and Stovall had been up for days, questioning Brudos, searching for evidence.

The black slip Brudos forced his victims to wear.

Salem Police Detective Jerry Frazier spotted this rope with its very distinctive knot in Brudos' garage, and thought it matched the knots found on the victims' bodies. Brudos offered Frazier this knot—which subsequently helped convict him.

The gun Brudos used to abduct his victims.

Brudos on his way to court. (Photo credit: Gerry Lewin)

"It's nothing," he said shortly. "They're charging me with carrying a concealed weapon."

"But *why*?"

He turned away. Darcie watched Jerry disappear behind a steel door, and then she took her children home.

— 14 —

Jerry Brudos, having lied to his wife again, was led back to his cell, past curious prisoners. He was still not particularly worried. He had expected the police would do something like this—but he was secure that they had no way to tie him into whatever they were accusing him of. He considered that they were just using a desperate ploy, hoping that they could keep him in jail.

He did, however, call Dale Drake and ask that he come to the jail. He was smart enough not to go through this without an attorney. Drake stayed the night at the jail. Later, years later, Jerry Brudos would insist that he had no lawyer in attendance. He would relate that other prisoners "beat the living hell out of me." He would also claim that he had been poisoned in jail. He had always seen things in his own way, shaped them until they fit him; he would view his incarceration the same way.

And yet, there was something quite challenging about his arrest. Jerry considered himself brilliant. He mentioned to several officers and to his lawyer that his I.Q. had been tested at 166—well over genius demarcation. (He had actually tested 105 on the Wechsler-Bellevue scale; possibly the lower figure could be attributed to stress.) He did not believe there was a cop in the country who could outsmart him, and he looked forward to the jousting that would take place in the coming interviews, confident that he would win.

Stovall waited downstairs to interview the prisoner. Stovall is one of the best police interrogators in the country, having refined it to an art.

"It's a cat-and-mouse procedure," Stovall explains. "Always, *always*, the investigating team must withhold facts that place the suspect at the scene of the crime. We know something about him, and he knows—or suspects—that, but he doesn't know what. We form a kind of dialogue. The interrogator is never hurried; he deliberately allows the suspect to lead him away from the main points—but never too far. If the suspect says something incriminating, we never pounce on it right away. We let it slide until we're ready, and only then do we come back to it."

Obviously, a great deal had happened between the times the dead and missing girls had disappeared and the time they were found. Only one living person would know those events—and Stovall was quite sure that the big man before him held all those secrets. He could see Brudos taking his measure, and he himself watched the suspect covertly, evaluating his attitude.

The man was cocky, and seemingly at ease. That was good. Cocky suspects are more likely to spill their guts than those more nervous—they yearn to brag and show off, almost heedless of the fact that they let vital bits of information slip out.

This man—Jerry Brudos—quite likely had things to tell that no man really wanted to hear . . . but not soon, and not without a sound foundation of dialogue.

Stovall would make himself available all weekend; he did not expect to glean much from this first interview. If Brudos should decide he wanted to talk, the interrogator never wanted to be more than five minutes away.

Outside the windowless interview room, one could hear male voices and a few fragments of sound from a small radio, droning out the results of the qualifying laps at the Indianapolis Speedway. Inside, alone with the suspect, Stovall waited out the long silences. Brudos seldom looked directly at Stovall, but the detective could detect no beading of sweat on his forehead, no acceleration of breathing as if the suspect felt panicky.

He almost seemed to be reveling in the attention, anxious for the game of give-and-take to begin.

Stovall asked only the easiest questions. Brudos' full

name. His address. Date of birth. Wife's name. Employment history. Vehicles available to him. It might have been an interview given for a new job.

But it wasn't.

"You never divulge," Stovall comments. "You merely suggest, and wait for the suspect to carry it a little further."

"It's a puzzle," Stovall said quietly. "How something like this—all of this—could have developed. So many women missing.

Brudos nodded slightly.

"It's very complex, shows a lot of planning."

Brudos shrugged.

"Do you have any theories? Any way to make sense of this?"

"My attorney would prefer that I don't go into that."

Stovall pulled back, veering off into a less potent subject. "You ever drive a car, other than your own? Or the Karmann Ghia?"

"I drive my mother's sometime."

There was something there, a flicker of disgust in Brudos' eyes. *This man did not like his mother.*

"What kind of a car is that?"

"Rambler, 1964."

"One of those blue jobs? They all seem to look like boats—nautical."

"No. It's light green."

"Do you want a cigarette? A cup of coffee?"

"I don't smoke. I seldom drink, either. No bad habits." Brudos smiled.

Stovall smiled back.

"I think I'll go back to my cell. Those cops woke me up when they arrested me. I worked hard all day."

Stovall stood obligingly and signaled for a jailer.

The first contact was a draw, and Brudos seemed to think that he had handled it well.

"I'll be around if you want to talk more," Stovall said easily.

He watched the big man shamble down the hall on his way back to jail, and knew he might have to wait hours—days maybe—but that Brudos would be wanting to talk again.

Stovall had a cup of coffee and began to organize what would become voluminous notes. In front of the prisoner, he would take few notes, but when he was alone, he would jot down everything that seemed pertinent, and index the answers. That way, he would have a starting point with each new confrontation.

Hours later, the word came from the jail: "He wants to talk again."

"Bring him up."

They began again. The first tentative innocuous remarks. Brudos did not like his cell. It was a "closet." The only window, by his own measurement, was four inches by ten inches and closed up. The light was turned off too much.

Stovall commiserated. "Jails aren't built for comfort."

"Do you know where my wife is?"

"She went home hours ago."

Stovall could detect real concern for the prisoner's wife; his attitude when he spoke of her was nothing like the loathing he evinced when he talked about his mother.

"How do you do this business?" Brudos asked. "I mean, how do you know things—if you have no proof?"

"It's a matter of our knowing some things and other people knowing other things—and eventually they usually come together and we get the whole picture."

"So you don't know everything going on, do you?"

"Nobody claims that. As I said, it's a puzzle. You think of somebody doing all of this . . . and you wonder. You have the pieces of the puzzle, maybe, but you don't have the box with the picture of what it's supposed to look like. You have a thousand-piece puzzle, and all you can do is put the pieces together by color to begin with. We separate the blues from the greens and the browns, for example. So we form the borders, and we keep working toward identifying other pieces—keeping the color scheme of things in mind. Blue. Green. Brown."

Brudos seemed to like that analogy. Stovall didn't

fill him in on the rest. The trial and the error and the hard work, and sometimes losing track of the most important piece because it hadn't fit when you first tried it. Gradually the whole picture always does begin to form. The crime-scene evidence, and the interviews, and the countless hours of follow-up reports.

"Without the picture, it sounds impossible to me," Brudos commented. "I guess you get discouraged."

"Not necessarily."

The silence yawned.

"I know you picked me up because you thought I was guilty of something or other . . ."

"You're charged with assault with a deadly weapon."

"Yeah."

"You're an electrician. Are you pretty skilled at that?"

"I guess you could say that. Electricity . . . electronics, that stuff."

"Who did you work for when you lived in Portland in 1968?"

"Osborne. . . ."

"You worked many places around Salem?"

"Over in West Salem, and out in Lebanon, and then in Halsey."

"That's a long commute."

"It's not bad—almost all freeway."

"You had a little trouble when you lived in Corvallis back in the fifties."

"I was a kid. They sent me out to the hospital here. That was a long time ago."

"Yes. You must have been in high school then."

Brudos shifted. "I can't see how you'd know if I did something . . . with those girls. I can't see how there'd be any way to prove it."

"Do you want to discuss that?"

Brudos shook his head and looked away. "Drake said I didn't have to talk about any of that. He's my attorney, and I think I should do what he says. Did you know I went to high school with him? At least, he says we did—he says he remembered my name because we were in the same homeroom. Small world, huh?"

Stovall nodded. Brudos was avoiding direct questions, and he was adroit at changing the thread of conversation. Stovall wasn't going to push him.

The rest of that interview went the same way. Every time the detective veered too close to something Brudos didn't want to talk about, the conversation switched gears. He saw that Brudos was dying to know what the investigating team had found but that he would not come right out and ask. Nor would the suspect offer any new information.

Again, they had come to an impasse. Brudos was returned to his cell.

They were to continue their abortive discussions for three days, and each new confrontation touched a little closer on the girls' murders. Stovall's notes were becoming more defined. He spent half an hour or more after each session correlating and indexing. Brudos *had* been in the vicinity of every abduction. That was clear. And he'd had the means. The guy was strong; his soft layer of fat hid power. Opportunity. Means. Motive? Motive was becoming more apparent, an underlying madness in a man who clearly detested his mother, and that hatred had ballooned until it included all women—all women except Darcie Brudos.

The mother—Eileen Brudos—seemed to still control her son as if he were only a child. The loan of her car, the frequent loans of money to a man who could not hold a job. Every time the suspect mentioned his mother, there was a concurrent tightening in his jaw in apparent loathing.

Stovall sensed that he himself had passed some kind of test. Brudos seemed to respect him, considered him a fit adversary. The suspect obviously saw himself as a major intellect, and it was essential that he accept his interrogator as someone worthy.

The dialogue had been formed. If it meant that Stovall would have to home in on a kind of madness, he was prepared to do that. And yet he dreaded the denouement of the puzzle almost as much as he sought it. He had to keep reminding himself that the helpless victims were long dead and beyond pain. Even so, whatever had happened would have to be relived in the quiet interview room. . . .

Shifts changed. First Watch. Second Watch. And then Third Watch, and it began again. Stovall drank too much coffee, grabbed fragmented bits of sleep, and took quick showers. Upstairs in his cell, Brudos slept too.

He did, in fact, sleep well. He had called Darcie and told her what she must do. She had always obeyed him, and he counted on that now.

Darcie Brudos was in a state of shock. She kept trying to work back through her mind to make some sense of what had happened. One minute they had been heading off to Portland for the holiday weekend with friends. She had been happy and relaxed, looking forward to three days with people she liked, to break up the gloom of her relationship with Jerry.

But the next . . . The police had moved up behind their station wagon so swiftly, their voices disembodied then behind the glare of flashlights in her face. They scared her, and they scared the kids. She was still scared, alone in the house.

She had no idea what Jerry might have done. She knew he had some guns, but as far as she knew, he never carried them around with him; they were for hunting or for trading. She wondered why the police would follow them halfway to Portland and stop them on the freeway for something like possession of a weapon.

She would not let herself imagine what else might be involved; she would not allow other thoughts to creep in. Jerry was strange, and he'd been stranger lately, but that was only because he was so sensitive. That was only because people—herself included—kept disappointing him. He was the father of their children. He was her husband.

She sat in the darkened living room and stared out at the cars that crawled down Center Street, seeing their headlight beams creep across the far wall.

When the phone rang, she practically jumped out of her skin. It was Jerry, calling from jail. He sounded like himself, a little tense, but in control. He would not wait to listen to her questions; he had something important for her to do.

"Darcie . . ."

"Yes, I—"

"Just listen. I want you to do something for me. I want you to go out to my workshop. There's a box out there, and it's got some old clothes in it."

"What kind of clothes?"

He paused. "They're women's clothes, just some junk I had out there. I want you to burn them. And there's a box of photographs there too. Destroy both those boxes."

"Jerry . . . *why*?"

"The police might try to use them against me. They're asking a lot of questions. Just go out there and get them and burn them."

She could not do it. There were so many things that Jerry wasn't telling her. In the morning she called Dale Drake and asked him what she should do. He told her it would be illegal for her to destroy anything that might be construed as evidence. "If you do, it might tend to incriminate *you*."

She didn't go out to Jerry's workshop at all; she was afraid to, and she was afraid to tell him that she hadn't done what he asked.

Instead, she took a few clothes for herself and the children and drove to Corvallis to stay with her parents. When they asked questions, she couldn't answer. She called Jerry's brother in Texas and told him Jerry was in trouble, but she couldn't answer his questions either.

She remembered the sight of Jerry dressed up in the bra and girdle, the photograph of him grinning, wearing the black lace slip and high heels, and the ones of Jerry lying on the bed in female lingerie.

Maybe that was it. Maybe that was against the law, and someone had found out.

— 15 —

Brudos wanted to talk again.

Jim Stovall stacked his notes carefully in an outer office and walked into the interview room. Jerry looked a little tired, but he wanted to continue their discussion. He was more anxious now to ferret out what the police knew.

"How would you know if I did it?"

"What exactly are you talking about, Jerry?"

"The girls. If you thought I killed those girls, how would you know anything if I didn't tell you?"

"Certain things we know. Certain things you know. . . ."

"What kind of things?"

Stovall was silent for a moment, and then he said slowly, "Well, for instance, if it ever came to pass that you know something about clothing . . ."

"Like what clothing?"

"Items of clothing found . . . items that seemed out of place."

"*My* clothing?"

"No."

"Clothing that was out of place?"

"Yes."

The answer popped out of the suspect's mouth swiftly—a slip, or deliberate? "You must mean the bra . . ."

Stovall kept his own breathing steady and forced himself to continue casually doodling on his scratch pad. The answer was right, an answer that no one but Karen Sprinker's killer would know. That black long-line bra with six hooks and eyes had been described to Karen's mother. And Mrs. Sprinker was positive that

Karen had never had such a garment. It was too big, and totally different from Karen's own bras.

Stovall would not pounce on the throwaway remark. If he did, Brudos might retreat and say nothing more. He would wait and let it drift back into the conversation later. He nodded slightly and went on to other areas. Brudos wanted to talk; he wanted to tell it all, but it had to be drawn out slowly.

They talked about the girl in the dorm in Corvallis; that was known to the police, and Brudos knew that. She was just "someone to talk to," and not his type.

What was his type?

"Women who dress nicely and wear high-heeled shoes. I like shoes."

Stovall agreed. "They look better than sneakers or flat heels, don't they?"

Brudos nodded enthusiastically. "A lot better. I try to get my wife to wear high heels all the time, but she says they hurt her back."

It was clear that talk of shoes excited Brudos and that he assumed that the detective had put no importance on the mention of the bra. "I collect shoes."

"Where would you get shoes? You mean you buy them?"

Brudos shook his head impatiently. "No . . . no. I take them from women."

"How would something like that be accomplished?"

"My lawyer doesn't want me to talk to you, you know."

Stovall nodded, and waited. He could see that a wall of lawyers wasn't going to stop Brudos from bragging.

"There was this one girl in Portland. Back a couple of years ago—maybe 1967. She lived out on South East Pine Street. I was working at Qeco-Osborne Electric Company then, and I was just driving around one day and I saw her. She was wearing a pair of high-heeled shoes. I guess I fell in love with her shoes. I started to follow her, and I noted the address of the apartment where she lived. I went back later—maybe it was early in the morning. It was dark. I didn't want her; I wanted her shoes."

"How would you get in to take her shoes?"

"I took off the window screen—it was already loose. I was only trying to get her shoes when she woke up and started to move. I had to choke her so she couldn't see me. She was wearing a two-piece pajama outfit. I unbuttoned the top and took off the bottoms and had sex with her. She was okay. She woke up when I finished, and I grabbed three pairs of her shoes—and a black bra—and left."

"Did you take anything else?"

He seemed surprised. He was not a thief. He only took underwear and shoes. "No, nothing else."

"That's how you collect your underwear and shoes?"

"Sometimes I find them on the clotheslines. Sometimes I have to go inside and steal them."

"Was that the black bra we were talking about—is that where you got it?"

"No, that was different. The one we were talking about was wide." Brudos held his hands six to eight inches apart to demonstrate. "It caught my attention on a clothesline in Portland a couple of years ago, and I took it."

"And you saved it—kept it someplace?"

"Yes. With the others."

Brudos apparently felt quite safe. They had talked of such a minor thing as stealing underwear from clotheslines, and he had explained away the rape in Portland as only something that happened almost "accidentally" as part of his "collecting."

Stovall had been careful not to evince shock or express judgment on any of the activities. The whole story of the long black bra would be more threatening to the prisoner, and he let it wait for the moment.

"While you were living in Portland, did anything else happen?"

"You mean the girl with the encyclopedias?"

Bingo. "Yes. Her name was Linda."

"She came to my house and I was out in the yard. I thought she was a boy at first—her hair was so short. She said she had an appointment with somebody at our house. I took her around to the rear door and into the basement and told her I wanted to buy the books."

Stovall waited. "Was anyone else home?"

"I told her we had company, but we didn't. My mother was upstairs with my little girl. She sat on a stool in the basement workshop trying to talk me into buying the encyclopedias. . . .

"I walked around behind her. There was a two-by-four about four feet long there. I hit her with it and she fell off the stool. She was unconscious. Then I choked her and she died."

Jerry Brudos had just admitted his first murder. Jim Stovall accepted it calmly, and Brudos continued describing the death of Linda Slawson.

"My wife was out, but my mother was there. I went upstairs and told her to get some hamburgers. I went back downstairs, and then I heard this friend of mine from Corvallis calling out to me."

"What was his name?"

"Ned Rawls. I went out the back door again and around to the front. I told him I was making nitroglycerin in the basement and I couldn't talk, and he went away. I went back to the basement and took the girl out from where I hid her under the stairs."

"Do you remember what she was wearing?"

It had happened eighteen months earlier. Stovall knew that if the woman could be found, there would be nothing left but her clothing and her bones. A specific description of clothing or jewelry would be important.

"Her outer clothes? No. She had a blue brassiere, slip, and girdle—and red panties. I dressed her and undressed her, like she was a big doll. I tried on some of my other things—from my collection.

"I couldn't keep her there. There was my mother and my wife, and they would have found out."

"So what did you do?"

"Early in the morning, about two A.M., I loaded her into the car and took her to a bridge over the Willamette. I took the jack out of the car so it would look like I had a flat, and I threw her over."

"She was never found."

"No. I didn't think she would be. I weighted the body down."

"With what?"

Brudos paused for a moment. If he answered, he would be really getting into it. And then he answered: "With the head of a car engine."

"Is there anything else you want to say about Linda Slawson?"

"I cut her foot off."

"You cut her foot off? When was that?"

"Just before I threw her over. I couldn't keep her, but that was a small part I could save. I had a hacksaw and I cut her left foot off because I'm right-handed. I took it home and put it in the freezer and used it for a photography model and to try shoes on."

"Do you still have it?"

Brudos shook his head. "I couldn't. The women might have found it. After a while, I weighted it down too and threw it in the river."

"Do you remember anything else about that girl? That would be Linda Slawson."

"She had a ring. A class ring from some school back east. A Catholic school, I think."

"She was not afraid of you?"

"No. She was just sitting there trying to sell me books, and then she didn't see me with the board. After I hit her, she was unconscious."

The floodgates were open, but there were three more cases—possibly others—to be got through. Jerry Brudos' demeanor had changed as he told of his crimes. He was cockier and more confident now. He had pulled off abductions that had baffled hundreds of police officers, and he seemed proud to be able to lay out the details of his plans.

It would be a long, long day.

"You know, Jerry, we're attempting to find out what happened to Jan Whitney. We found her car near the I-5, but we never did find her. Would you know what happened to her? It would have taken a lot of planning, I would think, to make a woman just disappear like that."

Brudos smiled slightly.

"Did you ever know Jan Whitney?"

"Not really."

"You encountered her in some way. Would that be it?"

Brudos said nothing. The time sequence was closer; it was almost as if Linda Slawson's murder was not as threatening because it was so far back in his memory. But Jan Whitney had been missing only six months.

"That's a long time back—back to last year," Stovall said. "A person could forget."

That annoyed Brudos, apparently. "I remember."

"You were living in Salem last November, weren't you? Were you working then?"

"I was working in Lebanon."

"That day Jan Whitney disappeared was a Tuesday. You worked that day?"

"Yes. . . . Her car was broken down on the freeway. I saw it on my way home that night."

"What color was it?"

"It was a red-and-white Nash Rambler. It was sitting on the shoulder about two miles south of Albany. She was standing there, and two guys. Two hippie guys."

That was a surprise to Jim Stovall. Jan Whitney hadn't been alone! If two men had been with her, they certainly hadn't come forward to aid in the investigation. But Brudos seemed adamant that there were two young men with her. "She was there with two other individuals? What did they look like?"

Brudos shrugged. "Hippies. They all look alike. Long hair. Young. Jeans and headbands. Kids."

"Were they with her, or had they come along?"

"I gathered that she'd given them a ride, and her car broke down and they didn't know how to fix it. I offered to fix her car, but I didn't have my tools with me. I gave the three of them a ride to Salem and let the hippies off at an on-ramp so they could go on north."

"She was willing to go on with you?"

"Sure. I said I'd take her back and fix her car. I drove to my house on Center Street and pulled into my garage. I told her to wait there in the car while I told my wife I was going back to fix her car, and she did. I told her my tools were in the house.

"My wife wasn't home. I came back and told the girl that I couldn't get into the house, that we'd have to wait a few minutes until my wife came home—made some excuse about where my wife was."

"Did you expect your wife home in a few minutes?"

Brudos shook his head. "Not for a couple of hours. She was over at her friend's house."

"What did you do then?"

"I got in my car and sat behind the girl. I said it was a funny thing to ask someone to close his eyes and try to explain how to tie a shoe. You know, without using your hands to show how, when you can't see."

Brudos gestured with his hands, and Stovall saw that his fingernails were bitten to the quick, like a child's hands can be. It looked peculiar on a grown man.

"And she did? She told you?"

"She looked at me and started using her hands, and I told her that wasn't what I meant. That she had to turn her head around and look toward the front and tell me what to do without moving her hands. So she turned around, and she's saying, 'You take the right lace and you pass it over the left and underneath . . .' and I took a mailman's leather strap I'd got from the house and made a loop over her head and pulled it tight around her throat. Then I opened the rear car door and put my end of the strap through it and closed it. She was pulled back and bent backward over the seat."

"She was dead, then?" Stovall asked quietly.

"She didn't move. She couldn't move. I went in the house to check to be sure my wife wasn't home, and she wasn't. I went back to the car, and she—the girl—was dead. I turned her around on the seat and had sex with her body from the rear."

Jim Stovall had fully expected that the killer he had sought was a sexual psychopath. Jerry Brudos was not the first psychopath he had encountered, but he was the most monstrous. He was a sadist and a necrophile, his sexual desires fulfilled by engaging in erotic acts with women who were either unconscious or dead.

Stovall felt sick; he could not betray his feelings or act on his natural desire to leave the room and get some fresh air. The process had begun. He was hearing what he had sought to hear when he began the dialogue two days ago. It seemed like two months.

"Did you dispose of Jan Whitney's body? I would wonder how you managed that."

"Not then. I took her into the workshop, and later I had sex with her again. I dressed her in some of my clothes collection and took pictures of her. I have a hook in my workshop, and I hoisted her up on a rope."

"You couldn't keep her there forever."

"No. I left her hanging there each day, and after work I would go out there and dress her and have sex with her. I was not sure what to do with her. I wanted something—something to keep."

"You had pictures."

"Something more. I thought I could make paperweights out of her breasts. I cut off her right breast and I was going to make a plastic mold and then I could make lead paperweights. I skinned out the breast and stretched the skin over a sawdust mound, and then I tacked the edges onto a board. I used plastic to make a mold, but it didn't work. I added too much hardener, and it didn't turn out like I wanted."

Jim Stovall thought of the few killers in history whose fetishes had extended to mutilation and subsequent preservation of the bodies. It was a blessedly rare phenomenon. Until Brudos, Ed Gein of Wisconsin was the best known—and the little recluse who had hated his mother so much that he had killed her and other older women and made vests of their dried flesh. But Ed Gein had been a lifelong bachelor, absolutely ruled by his hated mother; this man had a wife, children, an education, and a brilliance in his work. And still he recounted the acting out of his terrible fantasies in a voice as commonplace as if he were describing how to rewire a lamp.

Brudos' voice cut into Stovall's thoughts. "You guys almost caught me on Jan Whitney. I was scared to death."

"What do you mean?"

"The wife and I went to Portland around Thanksgiving, and I left the girl hanging in my shop. Some guy drove his car into my garage and left a hole in it. The police came out, and they wanted to get into the garage, but it was locked. That was close.

"When I got home, I found their card and so I took the girl out of the workshop and put her in the pumphouse in the backyard and covered her with a sheet of plastic. Then I called the cops and they came out and checked my workshop. They never suspected anything, and there was this wide-open hole there. If they'd shone a light in, they maybe could have seen her hanging there. . . ."

If only. If only. Those thoughts came up so often in a homicide investigation. If the victim had not gone where she had—if she had not somehow crossed the path of a killer ready to strike. If *this* had happened, then the tragedy would not have happened. For those who believe in fate, it is easier to fathom. If only Jan Whitney's body had been discovered in November 1968, then Brudos would have been stopped. Then Karen Sprinker and Linda Salee would be alive.

Stovall easily kept Brudos going on his monologue, so caught up was the prisoner in revealing his terrible scenario. "You did dispose of the body then?"

"I threw her in a river. I weighted her down and threw her in a river. The water was very high."

"Which river?"

"The Willamette."

"Where was that—at what point on the river?"

"I don't care to say."

"Was it in Portland?"

"No."

"Was it the Long Tom—and not the Willamette?"

"I told you it was the Willamette. That's enough. It was a long time ago. It doesn't matter."

Stovall wondered at Brudos' sudden reluctance; he would give the most minute and horrific details, and then balk at something that seemed simple. He seemed to believe that, without a body, he could not be convicted of killing Jan Whitney. He did not know that "corpus delecti" is not a human body at all, but rather "the body of the crime." He knew little of the law, obviously, despite his superior attitude.

"Was it at Independence?"

"I can't say."

Stovall mentioned other bridges in the Salem area, but he thought Brudos' reaction to the suggestion of the bridge at Independence was the most telling. No body had been found there, and it might never be after six months without discovery.

"Jan Whitney's car was not on the freeway when it was found. It was somewhere else."

"I went back and moved it after I had her hoisted up in my shop. I tied it to mine with a tow bar and pulled it into the rest stop at Santiam. I was going to get rid of it entirely, but I saw three state police cars while I was towing it—two going south and one going north. I couldn't take the chance that one of them might stop me and ask about her car. So I just towed it into the Santiam rest stop, locked it, and left it."

"What would you have used to weight Jan Whitney's body down? Whatever it was, it must have been effective."

"Scrap iron. I had scrap iron out in the pumphouse."

Jim Stovall considered the information he had elicited from Jerry Brudos thus far. He had two confessions—verbal confessions—on homicides whose victims might never be found. Jerry Brudos certainly had knowledge that no one else could have known; he had mentioned details that had been withheld from the news media. He knew the dates, the places, and the manner of death. Or did he? Without the bodies, no one could say what the manner of death had been. One thing was certain: Brudos' confessed acts against nature had grown increasingly violent. First the theft of undergarments and shoes, then the choking of women, then rape, and then murder.

The homicide of Linda Slawson had, according to Brudos, not involved rape—only the dressing and redressing of the body. Jan Whitney's body had been violated again and again after death. It was as if the obsessive perversions that drove Brudos grew like a cancer within him, demanding always new horrors to satisfy and titillate that malignancy.

With every sensational murder case, there are a half-dozen or more men who confess to the crimes. They want attention, a sense of importance at being, however briefly, in the limelight—or they gain some erotic stimulation from lying about the details of crimes they never committed.

At this point in the interrogation, Stovall had to look at the two confessions with suspicion. Ninety percent of him thought he had the right man, and he was positive he had the man who had threatened Liane Brumley and tried to abduct her. But Stovall had to be careful in correlating what the suspect had said about Whitney and Slawson. It was possible that Brudos was only a weirdo, a student of newspaper accounts of sexual crimes, who had concocted his own fantasy stories.

Each bit of information gleaned in the interview was thoroughly checked, even as Brudos' statements continued. Each time Stovall stepped from the room, he handed notes to Frazier and other members of the team for follow-up.

Brudos had said that Jan Whitney's car had been broken down on the I-5 on the evening of November 26. Frazier called the Albany station of the state police and asked them to check back through their logs during late November 1968 for a possible corroboration of that information.

"Yes," the answer came back. "One of our troopers noted a red-and-white Nash Rambler parked on the east shoulder of I-5 at seven minutes after ten P.M. on November 26—at milepost seventy, two miles south of Albany. No driver or passengers in the area. It was noted, and the trooper on the next shift would have tagged it for towing if it had still been there. But it was gone by the next shift."

That information fit exactly with what Brudos had said. That spot at milepost seventy was just about ten miles from the spot in the Santiam parking lot where the car was eventually located. Someone *had* moved it in the wee hours of the morning. . . .

Frazier did a tedious hand check through all the Salem Police department's accident reports for the Thanksgiving weekend of 1968. He found the report of a car that had skidded off Center Street into a garage at 3123 Center. Minor damage reported. Occupants not at home.

Frazier located the traffic investigator who had left his card at the little gray house and who had subsequently interviewed Jerry Brudos. Yes, there had been a hole in the workshop portion of the garage, a gap in the splintered siding. It had seemed a routine investigation, with nothing to make him suspicious. He had seen only a family home, a few children's toys cluttering the back porch. Nothing at all to indicate there was a virtual abattoir within the garage, a torture chamber. Brudos had seemed anxious to get the place fixed so the rain wouldn't get in. The officer had been in the garage and workshop to check the damage from the inside, and it had looked just like anybody's garage. No body. Nothing strange in there at all.

But of course by then Brudos had, according to his statement, hidden Jan Whitney's mutilated body in the pumphouse.

The facts were beginning to mesh perfectly with the suspect's almost unbelievable confessions.

There was something else that Brudos could not have known without having been there. The long-line black bra found on Karen Sprinker's body. The mention of that bra had been Brudos' first slip, the initial fissure in the wall the suspect had built up.

If Brudos had killed Karen Sprinker, she would have been his third victim, according to his own recital of facts. Each case had been a little worse than the one before. Jan Whitney had allegedly had one breast amputated; Stovall knew that Karen Sprinker's body had been missing both breasts.

The detective truly dreaded hearing the next confession, but he would have to listen. The dialogue was an established thing now, and the original duo of players would continue. There could be no substitution of interrogators.

— 16 —

"It was in March . . ." Stovall said. "When Karen Sprinker disappeared . . ."

"The twenty-seventh."

"Yes. A weekday. It always seemed to be on a weekday."

"I spent weekends with my family," Brudos said.

"Had you ever seen Karen Sprinker before?"

"No. It wasn't that girl who attracted me. She just happened to be there."

"Where would that be?"

"Meier and Frank, of course. Everybody knows that—it was in all the papers. I have clippings at home that say that."

"That's true. You weren't working that day?"

"I had a sick day. I had a bad headache in the morning, and I didn't go to work."

"You didn't stay at home, though."

"No. I was just driving around. I drove by Meier and Frank, and I saw this girl."

"Was it Karen?"

"I told you it wasn't."

Brudos was cocky now. He seemed proud of the fact that he had managed his crime in broad daylight in the midst of a crowd of shoppers.

"I was just driving around, as I said, and I saw a girl near Meier and Frank. She was wearing a miniskirt and high heels. It was about ten in the morning. I watched her and she went into the store. The way she looked, her clothing and her shoes, turned me on. I had to have her.

"I drove into the parking garage and I parked on the third floor. I looked for the girl in the miniskirt inside the store. I must have spent an hour or more looking for her—but she was gone. Maybe she went out another door or something. Anyway, I couldn't find her and I went back to my car. I mean, I was walking back toward my car when I saw the other girl."

"Karen Sprinker?"

"I guess so. I didn't know her name. She had on a green sweater and a matching skirt. I didn't like her shoes, but she was a pretty girl with long dark hair. I watched her while she locked her car and then came down the steps toward the door into the store."

The description sounded so familiar to Stovall. Of course. This was the way the investigating team had pictured Karen's abduction. Standing there in the empty parking garage, they had visualized the way it must have been—ghost images left behind, almost palpable in their intensity.

"She reached to open the door, and I grabbed her by the shoulder. She turned around, startled-like, and saw the pistol I was pointing at her. I said, 'Don't scream and I won't hurt you. Come with me and I won't hurt you.' "

"Did she scream?"

"Of course not. She said she would do whatever I wanted if I just didn't shoot her. She kept saying that—several times—as if she was trying to convince me. I walked her to my car and put her inside. Nobody was in the parking garage."

Brudos continued in his monologue, intent now on recreating what had occurred two months before. "I drove to my house and into the garage."

"Was your wife home?"

"No. She was over at her girlfriend's house. She was always over there visiting. The girl—Karen—was still telling me that she would do anything to keep me from shooting her. I asked her if she had ever had a man before, and she said 'No.' She said she was in her period. That was true; she was wearing a Tampax."

Stovall knew this was correct information, and a detail withheld from anyone but the investigating team.

"I raped her—there on the floor of my workshop."

"Did she resist you?"

"No, she was afraid of the gun. Afterward she said she had to use the bathroom, so I took her into the house and allowed her to do that."

"That would have been out the side door of the garage and through the breezeway there to the back door?"

"Yes. She didn't try to run away or anything. I still had the gun. Then I took her back out to the workshop. I wanted some pictures of her. I took some in her clothes, and some in her underwear, and some in underwear I had out there. I had her wear the black patent-leather high heels that I have, because hers were very plain and low. I took a lot of pictures."

Stovall thought of the brilliant, gentle girl, trying to reason with a maniac, believing that she could keep him calm by going along with his orders. She would have been so frightened, and yet hoping desperately that he would set her free when he had finished with her. If she had fought him, what would have happened? Maybe she would have had a chance while she was in the parking garage, or even when she walked from the garage to the house—only twenty feet or so from a busy street. Maybe not. And yet Stovall doubted that Brudos would have had the guts to shoot her where there was a possibility that someone would hear.

So many female victims made the mistake of thinking that reason can temper madness. The odds are always better if a woman screams and kicks and draws attention in a public place. If a rapist or kidnapper shows enough violence to approach a woman and attempt to take her away by force, there is every possibility that he will show no mercy at all when he gets his victim alone in an isolated spot. Captivity and torture are the thrust of his aberration. Pity and compassion have no place in the makeup of a sexual criminal.

Too late for Karen.

"I tied her hands in back of her and told her I had to do that to keep her from going away. She said that wasn't necessary, but I couldn't trust her. Then I put a rope around her neck. I had it attached to a 'come-along.'

"I swung the rope up on the hoist, and tightened it around her neck. I asked her if it was too tight, and she said it was."

Jerry Brudos, who had never had control over women, had been in absolute control of Karen Sprinker's life.

And he chose to end it.

"I gave the 'come-along' about three more pulls and it lifted her off the ground. She kicked a little and she died."

Stovall's hand tightened around his pen, but he betrayed no other feelings. It was far too late to help Karen; there was nothing to do now but see that this man was off the streets forever—that he would no longer have a chance to act out his sick fantasies.

Brudos described how he had violated the girl's body after death, after taking time out to go into the house to be with his family.

"I went back out later and had sex with her. Then I cut off both of her breasts to make plastic molds. I couldn't get the percentage of hardener right this time either, but they turned out a little better than with the girl from the freeway."

"Jan Whitney."

"Yes. Her. I dressed the girl from Meier and Frank—Karen—in her own cotton panties and the green sweater and skirt. But I used the wide bra instead of her own. I stuffed it with paper towels so it looked all right and so she wouldn't bleed on my car."

"Where did you get that bra?"

"From a clothesline in Portland a couple of years ago. No, wait. Maybe it was one that belonged to my wife. I have a lot of them, so I can't be sure."

"Did you keep Karen's body for several days—the way you kept Jan Whitney's?"

Brudos shook his head. "No. I waited until my wife and the kids had gone to bed, and I took off about two A.M. for the Long Tom River. I weighted the body down with a cylinder head I had for a car. I tossed her into the river on the upstream side."

"Where did you get the cylinder head?"

"I had the stuff around; I fix cars a lot."

"Where are the pictures you took of Karen?"

Brudos smiled, secure that he could count on Darcie's absolute obedience to his wishes. "Gone. They've all been destroyed."

The two men had been cloistered in the little interview room for a long time. Neither smoked, but the air was heavy—perhaps from the weight of the words that had been spoken. Outside, it was spring and the huge magnolia trees on the courthouse lawn opened their waxy white blooms. Parks around Salem were filled with picnickers, some of them on the banks of the Willamette River. Inside the jail complex, there was no season at all, and certainly no sense of holiday.

There was a break in the interrogation; what had been said was too horrific to continue on endlessly. There would be more; Jerry Brudos seemed consumed with the need to pour it all out. He showed no regret at all about what he had done; he whined instead about his cell and the food, and asked for his wife. He talked to Dale Drake, his attorney. What was said in that conversation was privileged communication, but Drake was pale and his jaw was set when he emerged from the conference.

"Did you get anything?" Stovall's fellow investigators asked the detective, and he nodded grimly. He moved to a worktable where he could transcribe what he had heard onto the yellow legal pad, pages and pages of unbelievable cruelty. So many victims who had never had a chance. He indexed, and he correlated, and he saw that all the pieces had fallen into place. All but Linda Salee's murder.

And that would be covered in the next interview.

Brudos ate. Stovall could not. An hour or two later, they began again. Slowly. Easing back into the intimate revelations.

"We're into April now, Jerry," Stovall commented. "Can you recall your activities in April?"

"I remember everything. I have an excellent memory."

"Linda Salee disappeared on April 23, a Wednesday. Would that be the first . . . activity that month?"

"No. You know about the girl on the rail tracks. That was Tuesday. Before that—on Monday—I went to Portland, and I went out to Portland State University . . ."

Were there more? Were there other girls who had not yet been found? It was possible. Considering all the rivers coursing through the state of Oregon, there could be other bodies drifting there, unknown to the investigators. Stovall waited.

"I went up there to find a girl. I saw one in the parking complex at Portland State. She was older, maybe twenty-two to twenty-four years old. I had the pistol—it wasn't real; it was a toy, but it looked real. She fought me. She grabbed for the gun and she tried to twist it out of my hand. She was screaming and she caught my finger in the trigger guard and damn near broke it. She was attracting attention, and I knew I had to get away from there. I managed to get loose of her, and I walked up to the next floor of the parking garage, where my car was—I didn't run because that would have made people suspicious. I got in and drove away."

He was a coward, obviously. Fight him in public, and he ran like a rabbit. Stovall wondered if the girl from Portland had any idea of what she had escaped.

"You drove on home, then?"

"Yeah. The next day, I was driving around in Salem and I saw this young girl on the Southern Pacific tracks. I showed her the plastic pistol and told her that she was to come with me. I had her by the shoulder and I pulled her between two houses. She said she could walk by herself. I had her almost into the car—I had my friend's car that day—when she balked. She took off running. There was some woman working in her yard, and the girl ran to her, and I got in the car and took off."

"Two days in a row, you struck out. That might have made you a little angry—a little disappointed."

"A little."

"You might have been afraid that you had been seen, that you could be identified by someone."

"No. I got away easily both times. I didn't worry."

"You plan well. You probably worked out another plan that would work."

"Yes. I always had another plan, a backup plan. I went back to Portland the next day."

"That would be the twenty-third, then?"

"That's right. I had a badge, looked just like a real police badge—you can buy them, you know. I bought it right there in Lloyd Center; it was a toy, but you'd have to look real close to be sure. I started looking for a girl."

"You found a girl?"

Brudos nodded. "I saw this girl in the parking garage. She was walking toward her car and she had her arms full of packages. I went up to her and showed her the badge and told her I was taking her into custody for shoplifting. I said I was a special police officer assigned to Lloyd Center and would have to take her downtown with me. She believed me, but she said she hadn't stolen anything—that she had the sales slips to prove it. But she came with me quietly. She didn't fight me at all. She just got in my car."

"Did she ask questions when you went by downtown Portland and got on the freeway for Salem?"

"No. It was funny; it was like she wanted to go with me. She didn't say anything at all. She just rode along nicely."

"You drove with her all the way to Salem? That would have meant she was in the car with you for an hour."

"That's right. I got to my house and I drove into the garage and closed the doors. I told the girl to follow me, and I started for the house. I didn't know my wife was home. She walked out on the back porch just as I left the garage. I held my hand back and warned the girl not to come out, and she stopped. My wife didn't see her. I told Darcie to go back into the house and stay there because I had something important to do in the shop.

"My wife said that dinner was almost ready, and I

told her I'd be in in a minute. Then I tied the girl up with a rope and I went into the house for dinner. The girl was out there waiting in the garage. My wife said she was going to the health spa that night and that a baby-sitter was coming. That was okay, because she wouldn't bother me out in my workshop."

"You're telling me that Linda Salee was out there in the garage alone while you went in and ate dinner?"

"Yes. But she was tied up. Funny thing, though. When I went back out there to check on her after I ate, she'd gotten loose of the rope. She hadn't tried to leave the shop, and she hadn't even used the phone out there. She was just waiting for me, I guess."

It *was* odd, Stovall thought. But there might have been a close time element; the woman might have struggled free just as Brudos walked in the door. More likely, she had been terrorized into immobility. Just as a mouse tormented by a cat will simply give up, unable to run any longer, paralyzed by fright and indecision.

Or perhaps it was all a delusion in Brudos' mind, his surface ego demanding that the women he kidnapped should find him attractive and would seek out his company.

There was no way to tell now.

"I got the leather strap out—the postal strap that I used on the woman from the freeway—and I put it around her neck and pulled her off her feet. She was a little woman—short and light. She turned around, kind of, and she said, 'Why are you doing this to me?'

"I pulled the strap tighter and she went limp. I put her on the floor and got on top of her. I think I was inside her when she died."

"She just waited for you in the shop? She didn't try to fight you at all?" Stovall asked.

"Well . . . after I went back out there, I guess she did fight me. I don't know why—because she'd been so quiet all the time coming down and when I first put her in there. She fought me pretty bad until I managed to get the strap around her neck. I didn't like her—the way she kicked and scratched when I told her not to."

It was clear that Brudos felt a great deal of resentment toward Linda Salee, the girl who had resisted him. She was the first one; the others had gone down gently, but this athletic little woman had tried to live, pitting her strength against the hulking killer. If she only had fought earlier . . .

Still angry, Brudos had chosen to punish Linda Salee after her death. Mercifully, it no longer mattered.

"I hung her up by her neck from the hook in the ceiling where I'd hung the others. I had this experiment I wanted to try, using electricity."

Stovall tensed inwardly. There had been those strange marks on Linda Salee's body, the tissue near her ribs showing evidence of burns—something that had baffled both him and Medical Examiner Brady.

"An experiment?"

"Yeah. Once I had her up on the hook, I took her clothes off—having the hook there made dressing and undressing them easier. I took these two hypodermic needles and I stuck them on each side of her rib cage, and then I had electric leads attached to the needles. Then I plugged in the leads to see what she would do—if she would dance, or what. It didn't work; it just burned her."

"You kept her there for a while?"

"One day and one night. I raped her again, but I didn't like her body. Her breasts were all pink—the nipples weren't dark like they should be; they just all blended in together I didn't cut them off because they didn't appeal to me. I made some circular paper cones and put them over her breasts to make plastic molds, but the epoxy set up hot and it didn't work. I wasn't able to get a really perfect mold from any of them. When you salt a breast down and dry it, it shrinks to about a third of its normal size. I'm sure there's a way to do it so it will work, but I never could."

Thank God he would not have another chance to try.

"When did you take the girl's body out of your shop?"

"The second night. I tied the overdrive unit to her and put her in the Long Tom."

Jim Stovall went over all the versions of the murders

again and again. He would approach the vital points from one angle, and then come back from another angle. The facts never changed; they were entrenched in the suspect's mind—as if he had cherished his secret killing games and relived them until he knew every facet of them perfectly.

The thought of what Jerry Brudos had done was so despicable that a normal man could scarcely contemplate it without feeling a sickness in the gut. Jim Stovall had no doubt at all that if Brudos had not been caught, he would have continued to kill month by month until he himself grew old and died.

Brudos was taken back to his cell, and Stovall walked past the reporters who had clustered around the jail all weekend, eager for a headline story. The Associated Press had got wind of the arrest in the dorm at Corvallis, and printed that. They did not have the name of the suspect, or any details; they only knew that something big was in the wind. They would get nothing at this point of the probe.

Stovall stepped outside and thought the air smelled wonderful, but he was exhausted after three days of the most intense and macabre interrogation he had ever participated in.

Still, he wondered if he could sleep.

—— 17 ——

The headlines came on Monday morning. On June 2, 1969, an anxious public pored over this slight information:

> Marion County District Attorney Gary Gortmaker announced this morning that Jerome Henry Brudos, 30, a Salem electrician, has been charged with first-degree murder in the death of an Oregon woman. The victim listed in the charge is Karen Sprinker, 19, of Salem.

District Attorney Gortmaker declined to give the press any further information. Nor would he say where Brudos was being held: public feeling ran hot and vengeful; in the old days when the area was Oregon Territory, a man suspected of the crimes that rumor attributed to Brudos would have been summarily hung by an angry mob. Oregon had become a "civilized" state where a man accused must go through the due process of law. And yet . . . Officials feared what might happen if they revealed Jerry Brudos' location.

"Due process" meant that there were many legal and investigative procedures to be accomplished. A search warrant for Brudos' home and workshop, for his vehicles, a further check on facts elicited through Stovall's interviews, and then formal arraignment. In the face of cruel madness, calm, sane steps must be taken.

Detectives checked with Portland police to see if there had been a rape complaint in 1967 that resembled the case Brudos had discussed—a sleeping woman being throttled and sexually attacked. There was. Portland police records indicated their case, #67-35144, had occurred on May 18, 1967—"Assault, Possible Rape." The victim, Joyce Lynn Cassel, had given a statement that correlated almost exactly with what Jerry Brudos had described.

She had lost three pairs of shoes and a black bra. When she had regained consciousness, she'd found her window screen had been removed and set aside. She lived in an apartment on South East Pine. She had not really seen her attacker, because she had been wakened from a deep sleep and attacked in a darkened room.

Had Janet Shanahan also been one of Brudos' victims? Stovall thought not. He had questioned Brudos about the woman murdered in Eugene and left in her car, and Brudos had appeared to be totally unfamiliar with that case. Since he had freely admitted the other four homicides, there was no reason to think he would omit that case from his smug recital. He had also looked blank when Stephanie Vilkco was mentioned.

Brudos balked at reducing his verbal statements to written form, as if he felt his words had no substance that could harm him if they were not down in black and white in a formal statement.

There was now probable cause for a search warrant. Until the verbal statements, probable cause could not have been proved absolutely. A search warrant is a precise document; the items sought must be listed. The preservation of citizen rights in America does not allow lawmen to swoop down upon premises to seek out whatever may be there; the officers must list evidence they seek before they can obtain a search warrant. And if they should find items outside the sphere of an original search warrant, the premises must then be secured until an additional warrant is issued.

At this point, Stovall was able to list items that might well be found in the Brudos home: pictures, underwear, shoes, auto parts, copper wire, rope, the hook in the workshop ceiling, the "come-along," a leather postal strap, possessions belonging to the victims—and possibly even the molds made from the victims' breasts. Brudos had apparently not suspected that his arrest was so near, and the man who had hoarded all manner of bizarre paraphernalia might well have failed to dispose of it.

The first two elements of a solid case were now present. The circumstantial evidence. The confession. And still, there was a third element yet to be discovered: the physical evidence.

The physical evidence went back again to the placard over Jim Stovall's desk: "THE ELEMENTS OF SCIENTIFIC PROOF MUST BE PRESENT TO ESTABLISH AND SUBSTANTIATE A SCIENTIFIC CONCLUSION."

Marion County Circuit Court Judge Val D. Sloper issued a search warrant for the premises of the Brudos home early Tuesday morning, June 3. Armed with the search warrant and accompanied by Attorney Dale Drake and Larry Brudos, the defendant's brother, a group of investigators met at the gray shake house on Center Street. Larry Brudos unlocked the doors, and Stovall, Frazier, D.A. Gortmaker, and Lieutenant Robert W. Pinnick of the state crime lab and his assistants entered.

Nothing had been destroyed. Darcie Brudos had disobeyed her husband overtly for the first time in their marriage. And so all the grotesque tools of Jerry Brudos' crimes remained.

The men worked carefully, moving with excruciating slowness through the empty structures, a foot at a time, and then further once they had determined that they had obtained all evidence from each portion. They could not risk destroying evidence with a single thoughtless step. They photographed constantly, preserving the original appearance of the home and workshop.

Given other circumstances, many of the tools and much of the equipment might be considered ordinary. Given *these* circumstances, they took on macabre meaning.

There was a hook in the workshop ceiling; there was a thirty-foot three-sixteenth-inch rope and a "come-along" to winch an object upward. There was a leather postal strap with a cinch. There was more nylon cord. There were a vise and a locked tool chest. There were hundreds of keys, including a key ring in a brown case bearing numerous keys that seemed to be for cars and for house locks.

The searchers observed full scuba gear and fins, and reloading equipment for ammunition. They found a chest full of women's shoes—including spike patent-leather heels, other high heels, and a pair of low, laced shoes. There were ashes in a green plastic waste-basket that looked to be the residue of burned film or photographs.

There was a large blue shag rug on the floor of the workshop, a rug that seemed out of place in the area.

The investigators moved on to the main house and up into the dusty attic; it smelled of sun-baked wood, and cobwebs wafted in the slight breeze from the open door.

Most of Jerry Brudos' collection was in the attic. There were forty pairs of high-heeled shoes in all sizes from four to ten. White shoes. Brown shoes. Red shoes. Calf. Suede. Straw. Patent-leather. Open-toed sandals. Pumps. All of them slightly worn, and some of them curved to the shape of their original owners' feet.

And of course there were soft piles of undergarments, stolen by Brudos over the years, all the thefts managed when Brudos' compulsion gripped him. They found fifteen brassieres—fancy bras of lace and satin and sheer black nylon, and more utilitarian bras of cotton. They ranged in size from 30 A to 38 D. Some still smelled faintly of perfume; some were freshly laundered.

There were lacy slips and panties. There were dozens of girdles, all of them small-sized.

Some of the dust in the attic was thick and untouched, and there were clear spots where the big man had crouched as he pawed through his treasures, stimulating himself with his fantasies—all of this part of his hidden sex life.

The house itself seemed the home of an average young family—the children's toys still scattered where they had been left when Darcie Brudos abandoned the house to take comfort with her family. The kitchen was neat; there was still food in the refrigerator. But over the counter there was a roll of brown paper towels—towels that would prove to be identical in class and characteristics with those wadded lumps taken from the black bra Karen Sprinker wore.

In the living room, Criminalist Pinnick ran his hands along a high shelf over the fireplace. He touched an object and lifted it down.

It was a metal mold, formed in an exact replica of a female breast. The breast was full, and perfectly shaped. It was too perfect to have been fashioned from clay.

It was real.

There were photos on the shelf too—pictures of Brudos in a black lace slip.

When a further search of the house netted nothing more of evidentiary value, the men returned to the shop. They looked in a dim corner of the shop and saw—on a bench there—another breast mold. This breast was small; it had obviously come from a different source than the lush mold in the living room.

It looked real too—resin had coated human flesh, and taken on its form.

The toolbox lock was forced open. There were tools in the lower portion of it. In the upper-right-hand drawer there was a thick packet of pictures. Pinnick lifted them out carefully.

"Oh, my God . . ."

The investigators saw the glossy black-and-white shots, the pinups of a madman. Jan Whitney and Karen Sprinker—helpless in the lens of their captor.

It was deathly quiet in the shop as Pinnick slowly revealed each photo, holding them by the edges where no fingerprints could cling. The men gazed at the pictures, feeling a sense of personal intrusion on the privacy of the lost girls. Not one of them spoke; it was an experience they had never had before, and hoped devoutly never to have again.

There was a picture of a nude woman suspended from the ceiling by the damnable hook and its intricate pulley arrangements. Her face was obscured by a black hood. It would prove to be the body of Jan Whitney.

That would tie in with the verbal statements given to Stovall. Jan Whitney had not lived to get out of

Brudos' car, had died there with the leather postal strap around her neck.

Karen Sprinker had endured captivity in this very workshop. She stared mutely into the camera, and it was almost impossible to describe the expression on her face. Fear, yes. But something more—a kind of resignation, as if she had detached herself from the proceedings, as if her essence was gone and only her body submitted to the demands of the man behind the camera.

She wore different garments in the pictures. A bra and girdle that had not been her own. Another shot with a different brassiere and girdle. There was a photo where she wore only panties, and another where she had on just a bra. Her feet were encased in the spike-heeled black patent-leather pumps; her own plain flats rested on the fluffy blue rug.

"Damn him," one officer breathed. "Damn him."

Yes, damn him.

There was a black three-ring binder full of more photographs, variations on the other pictures. Many, many photos of nude female torsos, their heads snipped away by scissors.

It was obvious that all the pictures had been taken in the garage workshop; the blue shag rug showed in all the photos, and the Craftsman tool chest could be seen just behind the victims. It seemed impossible to think that Jerry Brudos could have held his captives here, torturing them and then killing them within feet of neighboring homes, just a breezeway removed from his own home. Yet the pictures established that. They substantiated the terrible confessions he had made to Jim Stovall.

Why hadn't the girls screamed for help? It seemed incomprehensible that they had not. And yet there is an explanation. There is profound shock in any kidnapping or hostage situation, a kind of denial. *This can't be happening to me.* Torn from their normal activities in situations that seemed safe, Brudos' victims had to have been instantly plunged into ultimate fear and denial. Studies done of prisoners in concentration camps—the survivors—elicited the theory that those who survived were the individuals who were able to override their shock and terror early on. Instead of "this can't be happening," they knew that it *was* happening, that it was true—and they fought back. Those who could not deal with reality, however terrible it was, died.

And so had Linda Slawson and Jan Whitney and Karen Sprinker and Linda Salee. Before they had time to accept their danger, they were killed.

The investigators had found so many pictures, and they found too the ashes of what seemed to be burned photographs, charred bits of proof sheets in the waste-basket and in the backyard. What had those pictures shown?

Lieutenant Pinnick spotted the corner of still another photograph, a photo caught between a work-bench and a wall. He pulled it out of the spot where it had apparently been overlooked.

It was an awful picture. A girl's body, clothed in a black lace slip and panties with garters, hung suspended from the ceiling. The camera angled up to her crotch—reflected in a mirror on the floor. The ropes swirled surrealistically, and the girl's muscles were relaxed. Her face didn't show, but clearly, she was dead.

"Look," Stovall said quietly. "Look at the bottom."

"What *is* that?"

"It's him."

It was. In the lower corner of the photo, there was the frozen image of a killer, caught unawares in the mirror. Brudos had photographed himself as he focused on the body of his victim, capturing his own lust-filled, slack face. He would not have dared to keep such a picture. But he had apparently lost track of this one last print when it slipped behind the work-bench. It was as if an unseen hand had secreted it there so that justice would be done.

The monster had photographed himself at the apex of his madness.

The searchers had been in the house and garage for hours, and they were finally convinced they had found all that they had sought. They cleared the property after changing the locks, and left it cordoned off with ropes and signs that forbade trespassing. All the physical evidence found was removed to the state crime lab for testing and evaluation.

Without the rest of it, that single picture would be enough. There was no way Jerry Brudos could explain that away, no chance for him to call back his confession. He had killed, and he had photographed himself in the very midst of his killing frenzy.

There was the matter of the hundreds of keys Jerry Brudos had collected. Where were the locks that they fit? Was there still more corroborating physical evidence among them that would tie him to his victims? Checking them all would be a monumental task, but Stovall, Frazier, and Daugherty did it.

The three investigators went first to McMinnville, where Jan Whitney's Rambler was in storage. The keys on the brown leather key ring opened the trunk of that car. Next they tried the ignition, and the lock turned. To be absolutely sure, the detectives installed a new battery in the Nash and tried the key again.

The engine turned over immediately.

The other keys did not work in Jan Whitney's McMinnville apartment. But the probers learned that Jan had lived previously in an apartment building near Portland State University. They had to hurry; even then, the buildings were being torn down to make way for a freeway. They located Jan's old apartment and found it had not yet been slated for the wrecking ball. Just in time. Two of the keys they had found worked. One opened the main entrance to the apartment building, and the other opened the apartment door to the unit where she had lived. They removed the locks, and those mechanisms, along with Jan Whitney's car, became three more items listed in the growing inventory of physical evidence.

Ned Rawls, Jerry Brudos' friend who had worked on cars with him for years, came to the state crime lab. Before he was shown the engine head that had been tied to Karen Sprinker's body, Rawls described to Lieutenant Pinnick a General Motors head that he had worked on with Brudos in early 1969. Several valves had been bad on the part, and Rawls remembered which of them had needed to be reground. To the nonmechanically minded, an engine head is an engine head; to Ned Rawls such parts were highly individual units. He told Pinnick where each flaw would be if this was the head that he and Brudos had worked on, which Brudos had kept at his house on Center Street.

Pinnick noted Rawls's specific descriptions. And then the two men went to where the engine head in question was stored. When the grease covering was wiped away, *every single specific detailed was present.*

It was another piece of physical evidence that was well-nigh irrefutable.

— 18 —

Salem attorney George Rhoten, one of the finest legal minds in Oregon, had joined the Brudos defense team when Jerome Henry Brudos was arraigned on June 4, 1969. He was still charged with only one murder, Karen Sprinker's, but charges in the Whitney and Salee cases were filed within a week.

Rhoten and Dale Drake had seen "the picture." A defense team composed of F. Lee Baily, Percy Foreman, Melvin Belli, and Clarence Darrow himself could not have formulated a defense on the basis of total innocence after seeing that.

Nor did Rhoten and Drake try. When Judge Sloper said, "You are charged with first-degree murder in the death of Karen Elena Sprinker. How do you plead?" Jerry Brudos answered, "Not guilty, and not guilty by reason of insanity."

Was Jerry Brudos insane, and insane under the law? According to the M'Naghten Rule, the legal guideline in most states in America, a defendant must be proved to have been unable to determine the nature and consequences of his act *at the time of the commission of the crime*. In layman's terms, had Jerry Brudos known the difference between right and wrong when he killed his victims?

Since no psychiatrist has ever been present to observe a killer at the time of his crimes, psychiatric evaluation must be done sometime after those crimes. The doctors' value judgments must be done then in retrospect, an imprecise and iffy method—but the only way possible.

One basic rule of thumb used by a prosecuting attorney to convince a jury that a defendant was *not* insane

161

during the crime is to show that he made efforts to cover up his crimes and to escape arrest. The only shoo-in for mental commitment rather than prison is the killer who is found babbling nonsense next to the corpse of his victim.

That doesn't happen often.

Jerry Brudos made elaborate preparations before his crimes, plotted them with cruel cleverness, and hid his guilt deftly thereafter. And still, the details of his crimes were so perverse that it was hard for some to believe he was, indeed, sane.

The teenage Jerry Brudos had been dismissed from an Oregon state hospital on the supposition that he only needed "to grow up." Well, he had grown up, and during all those years his perversions had multiplied and grown to grotesque proportions. Now seven different psychiatrists would interview Brudos separately and present their conclusions to the court. Drs. George R. Suckow, Gerhard Haugen, Roger Smith, Guy Parvaresh, Ivor Campbell, Colin Slade, and Howard Dewey examined the defendant individually.

They observed a man who was agitated and tense now; Brudos could not sit still for an interview, but rose frequently to stride around the interview room. He often stared at objects in the room with intense scrutiny. His fingernails were bitten to the quick.

Brudos characterized himself as a loner, and yet he seemed quite affable and talkative. He spoke with grandiosity and immaturity, and peppered his conversation with unnecessary detail, avoiding issues.

On an emotional level of response, he seemed quite normal—except when he talked of the deaths of his victims. He showed no emotion at all then. No remorse. He recited his litany of murder time and time again for each psychiatrist and each psychologist, and they all saw it—he was not sorry his victims were dead. Their lives were negligible to him.

Brudos described himself to one of the doctors: "I'm a friendly person who would give you the shirt off my back if you ask for it." And yet, a few minutes later in the examination, the defendant said: "I act the way I do because everybody takes advantage of me."

He had difficulty correlating dates in his past life with events, perhaps blocking out a childhood that had been miserable. Brudos' dislike of his mother was apparent to all the men who examined him. He loved women's clothing, but he declared he had never worn his mother's clothing—had never even thought of it. Her shoes were ugly. She favored his brother . . . always. She always made *him* take second place.

Jerry Brudos' hatred for his mother seemed to color all his thinking, and examiners detected a secondary hatred for all women—except Darcie.

"She won't dress up like other women do, and that makes me feel sorry for myself," he said with tears in his eyes. "But that's the only thing wrong with her."

Jerry Brudos cried—yes—but he cried for himself. When he talked of killing the four young women, his voice was flat and precise:

" . . . I stuffed the black bra with paper—because she was bleeding so much and I didn't want to get blood in my car."

". . . her breasts had pale pink nipples and they didn't show up well so I didn't take any pictures. I couldn't get a good cast of them, so I threw them away. Then I threw her in the river."

"I had sex with her and strangled her at the same time with the postal strap."

Hours-long interviews during which Jerry Brudos cried for himself, and for his wife—but never for his victims.

Asked to describe the sort of person he was, Jerry Brudos put forward some thoughts:

"I don't like to be told what to do. I live in a world full of people, but I feel all alone. I don't know if I knew right from wrong at the time of the deaths of those girls, but I know I didn't think about it. The thing that bothers me most right now is that I'm stuck here and that means I can't maneuver or work things out for myself. Before this, I could always control things and plot out what moves I wanted to make."

Jerry asked for treatment in a hospital. He felt sure he could become a useful member of society and raise his own children. . . .

It was obvious, however, that Brudos had never before sought out treatment for his mental problems; he had given the idea lip service only when he was trapped.

Jerry Brudos was given an electroencephalograph to determine if his bizarre fantasies were the result of brain damage, and he tested normal in brain function. He tested above average in intelligence and cognitive thinking.

He was not insane under the law. Not one of the seven doctors found him to be psychotic. They deemed him fully able to participate in his defense.

Dr. Guy Parvaresh summed up his evaluation of Jerry Brudos in a letter to Brudos' attorneys:

In psychiatric examination, he was obviously anxious, agitated, and depressed. He cried frequently, saying he was sick and that he could not have help. Throughout the detailed discussion of the crimes, he appeared very preoccupied, emotionally detached, and quite certain that "These things had to be done." There was a prevailing impression throughout the interview that basically this man had been threatened all his life with his emotional and physical existence—so much so that he has developed a well-organized paranoid thinking in that at no time after he began to get involved with a crime would he have doubt as to whether or not he should proceed. "There was no doubt they [the murders] had to be done whether I wanted it or not."

In general, I did not find any evidence of a psychotic process or evidence of perceptual disturbances. His cognitive processes are well-maintained, and he is able to give details of past and recent events. Based on clinical assessment, his intellectual capacity is above average. He shows poor and faulty social judgment and certainly has no insight into his basic emotional problems. It is my clinical opinion that Mr. Brudos understands the nature of the charges against him and can assist in his own defense. This man has a paranoid disorder and his behavior is a product of this disorder. Despite this, I believe he can differentiate between what is morally and socially right and wrong. A review of his past and the current examination make me believe this man is a menace to himself and society.

Dr. George R. Suckow, examining Jerry Brudos for the state, said virtually the same things in slightly different words:

Overall, this man describes a history going back to childhood of progressively increasing assaults upon young females, starting with fetishism for shoes and undergarments in very early childhood. One is reminded of the person who writes bad checks and does not get caught and then continues, getting worse and worse because no one draws a line showing him where appropriate behavior begins. At the point where he first came to Oregon State Hospital, essentially a line was drawn and for several years, if Mr. Brudos is to be believed, he reverted to fetishism only—but he ultimately began to progress and require increasingly bizarre things for sexual gratification. Interestingly, his sexual relationship with his wife, by his report, deteriorated over the past two years until recently it has simply been a mechanical act on her part at his insistence and not particularly satisfying to either.

Running throughout is a consistent thread of hostility toward his mother which generalizes to most women—but apparently not his wife at an overt level. On all three occasions that Mr. Brudos has requested psychiatric help, he has been in difficulty with the law. It is interesting that in the intervals between, when no one is after him, he does not require help. Though he does describe some rather elaborate fantasies of a sadistic nature toward women in particular, none of these is extensive enough or involved enough to qualify in my opinion as being delusions, since he clearly understands that they are not real, and even will discuss them in terms of how impractical they are.

In my opinion, Mr. Brudos has been aware of the nature and consequences of his actions on each and every one [crime] of which we spoke, and further he has been aware that they were wrong in the view of others.

In my opinion, his diagnosis is 301.7, Antisocial Personality, manifested by fetishism, transvestism, exhibitionism, voyeurism, and, especially, sadism. It is further my opinion that he is an extremely dangerous person to young females when not in confinement and, finally, it is my opinion that he shows little evidence of treatability, if any, for his personality disorder.

In the convoluted medicalese of the psychiatrist, Jerome Henry Brudos was quite sane, and eminently dangerous.

In the language of the man on the street, he was a monster. He would always be a monster.

Darcie Brudos never went back to live in the house on Center Street. Emotionally, she could not bear to; after reading the papers and seeing the story of her husband's alleged crimes featured on the news channels from Portland, she could not imagine living in the house again. It was a moot point anyway, because she was almost out of money and couldn't pay the rent.

She was led through the police barrier and allowed to pack her clothes and the children's, to pick up a few toys. Almost everything else had been seized for evidence, even her records. Everything. She was told that she could have some of the things later—if they proved to have no importance in the case.

Darcie and the children went first to her parents' home in Corvallis, but there wasn't much room there. Her parents agreed to care for Megan and Jason, and Darcie moved in with a cousin.

She talked to the psychiatrists, trying to answer

their questions. "He was always sensitive," she told them. "And he was strange. I was afraid of him."

"Why were you afraid?"

"Because I was all he had, and if I crossed him, I didn't know what he would do."

She answered questions about her sex life, her perceptions of what Jerry had been doing. And always she remained in shock—unable to assimilate the horror of it all. She had not known.

She had not known.

Jerry wanted her to visit him all the time. He wanted the children to visit. She went to see him, and he seemed the same—but nothing was the same, and nothing would ever be the same again. She didn't know what the police had found in Jerry's workshop, and he wouldn't tell her anything about it. But it had to be something or they wouldn't have charged him with killing Karen Sprinker and the other girls.

Darcie had nightmares, and woke with her nightgown soaked with perspiration. Her daytime thoughts weren't much better. The papers were saying that young women had been murdered in Jerry's workshop.

She could avoid visiting him for only a week or so, but then he called and was so insistent that she come. She went, but she wouldn't take Megan, no matter how he argued about it.

She wrote him a letter:

I'll be seeing you today in about four hours. Sweetheart, I hope you will forgive me for not bringing the kids today. Please understand, because it is tearing me apart, but I really feel I'm right. Megan knows what happened, but she doesn't understand. She gets tears in her eyes every time she talks about you.

Darcie Brudos

Darcie had always been easily swayed by her husband's arguments. He had controlled her life for almost eight years, telling her what to do and where to go. He did not seem angry with her that she'd failed to burn the things in his shop—maybe he didn't know. It was still very, very difficult for her to turn her back on him.

Like all the other victims, Darcie was shocked by the suddenness of the disaster that had befallen her. She too kept thinking: "This can't be happening to me."

—— 19 ——

On June 26, 1969, the subpoenas went out for a preliminary hearing before Jerry Brudos stood trial. The trial would be a long one, according to rumor. There were more charges now, and more victims listed. The initial list of potential witnesses included: Dr. Robert Paschko, the Salem dentist who had identified Karen Sprinker's body from dental X rays; Salem policemen Lieutenant Elwood "Hap" Hewitt, Sergeant Jim Stovall, and Detective Jerry Frazier; state policemen Lieutenant Gene Daugherty, Sergeant William Freel; Dr. William Brady, State Board of Health—the medical examiner; and Dr. Lucas Sprinker, Karen Sprinker's father. In addition, Ned Rawls's name was on the roster—Jerry Brudos' friend who had stumbled unaware into the middle of Brudos' first murder, and been turned away with a hurried lie about nitroglycerin.

Rawls had told Stovall and Daugherty about the trips to junkyards with Brudos to buy auto parts. He had also mentioned how strong Jerry Brudos was. "He could take all the weight of a three-hundred-pound freezer and never sweat. I'm strong, but his strength exceeds anything I've ever seen."

The witness list was growing longer, and Brudos' attorneys, George Rhoten and Dale Drake, foresaw a terrible macabre circus in court. They had their psychiatrists' evaluations and the reports of the state's psychiatrists. They knew that the insanity plea would not hold up; Jerome Brudos had been adjudged sane within M'Naghten's parameters. They did not relish such a trial—either for their client or for the victims' families, who would have to go through the ordeal.

Jerry Brudos had talked quite openly with Rhoten

and Drake, going over the murders, albeit a trifle less specifically than he had with Jim Stovall and the psychiatric evaluators. They were convinced almost from the beginning that their client was guilty of murder. He had told them so himself.

A criminal defense attorney works within restrictive bonds—both legal and ethical. He cannot reveal what his client has said to him in privileged communication. Yet he cannot misrepresent or falsify to the court. No responsible criminal defense attorney would seek to free a man of Brudos' killing propensities. When Rhoten and Drake had reviewed the possibilities of a defense from every angle, they saw that the *only* way to try for a not-guilty defense was to pursue a not-guilty-by-reason-of-insanity plea. They had approached Brudos with their conclusions, and he had not been particularly amenable to their advice. An insanity plea warred with his vastly overrated perception of his superior mental abilities. He argued that it would demean him to be portrayed as "crazy," and they countered that it would save him from prison. And so they had convinced him and entered original pleas of not guilty, and not guilty by reason of insanity, but Brudos had gone along only grudgingly, taking still another opportunity to remind Rhoten that he, "the crazy man," had an I.Q. of 166, that he was close to or surpassing genius.

Now, toward the end of June 1969, Rhoten and Drake found themselves between a rock and a hard place. Not a single psychiatrist or psychologist could testify that Jerry Brudos was insane at the time of his crimes—or at present. Whatever basis there might have been for an insanity defense had crumbled as the psychiatric reports came in.

The defense attorneys had a client whose burgeoning ego made him resistant to suggestion. And still they had to counsel him that he must now change his plea to one of guilty—or risk being flayed in court with the specific revelations of what he had done. If the details of his crimes came out in open court, he would be vilified by the media.

There was no question of the death penalty; it had

been outlawed in Oregon years earlier. The last killer
to die in the gas chamber in Oregon was Albert
Carnes. He was executed in the early 1950s for the
ax murder of a widow in her eighties named Litchfield.
A woman had been *sentenced* to die for the murder of
her lover's two small children in the 1960s—but emotion ran so high at the thought of the execution of a
woman that then-Governor Mark Hatfield commuted
her sentence to life in prison. (She was paroled in
1985.) Jerry Brudos did not have to worry about being
put to death for his crimes.

In the last week of June, George Rhoten and Dale
Drake had an hours'-long conference with Jerry Brudos.
They explained to him that he would undoubtedly be
incarcerated—either in a mental hospital or in the
state prison—and that, given their knowledge of the
facilities at the Oregon state mental hospital, he might
fare better in prison.

"Jerry, you will have to be separated from society—
both for your own good and for the good of society.
Do you understand that?"

Brudos nodded.

"I don't consider that you are insane," Rhoten said.
"And neither do the experts."

Brudos answered that he did not think he was insane or that he lacked any mental capacity to participate in decisions about his case.

"Mr. Drake and I are obliged to extend you every
legitimate defense that can be brought to bear on your
behalf. You are entitled to the constitutional guaran-
tees that are afforded defendants. But you have told
me certain things you say are fact, and you have told
me that what you told Dr. Suckow was true." (Brudos'
statements to Suckow were detailed and damning—as
much as or more than the statements made to Jim
Stovall.) "You have told me that what you told Sergeant Stovall can probably be used against you, and I
feel there is independent evidence strong enough to
convict you."

They talked for many hours, discussing over and
over again the possibility that an insanity plea would

fail, and the tremendous amount of physical evidence that the police had that was incriminating to Brudos.

Brudos was hesitant to plead guilty. He had been so sure that he would beat the police and the court.

"Now, Jerry Brudos," Rhoten said quietly, "you have told me that these things were done, and I believe you. I believe that you're telling me the truth, but I want to have some further corroboration. I want to know, in my own mind, whether or not there is something, by some quirk, that you are telling me to mislead me, so I am going to ask that this physical evidence be shown."

And so the two attorneys representing Brudos went to the evidence room and looked at the pictures, the rope, the breast molds, the leather postal strap, all of the wealth of damning evidence that had come from Brudos' home or had been attached to the victims' bodies in the river.

A miasma rose from the clothing, permeating the room. As they gazed at the evidence, it was difficult for Rhoten and Drake. At length, Rhoten returned to his client and said, "Well, this is correct; these facts are true."

There could be no denying that all Brudos' confessions were true—not after seeing his insanely lustful face in the photograph with one of his victims' bodies.

"I would like to talk to my wife—before I make a final decision to plead guilty," Brudos said.

Drake left the interview room and made arrangements for Darcie to be brought to the jail. Pale and trembling almost imperceptibly, Darcie walked into the room an hour later.

When she was through talking to her husband, she had no more illusions. It was over. Her marriage. Her life, it seemed. She had no home for her children. She had no money.

Jerry was guilty of murder, and he was going to say so in court.

She did not know what she was going to do.

— 20 —

If Salem courtroom observers expected to spend a good part of their summer in the Marion County Courthouse hearing all the details of Jerry Brudos' crimes—closeted there in the isolation and drama of a shocking murder trial—they were to be disappointed—at least for the time being.

There would be no trial for Jerry Brudos.

Attorneys George Rhoten and Dale Drake notified Judge Val Sloper that they had a motion to entertain in the late afternoon of June 27, 1969. Only a few of the principals gathered there in the quiet courtroom: Judge Sloper, Rhoten, Drake, District Attorney Gary Gortmaker, Jim Stovall, Gene Daugherty—and, of course, Jerry Brudos himself. Brudos, who had heretofore taken direction from no other human being, had listened to the sage advice of his attorneys. Going in, he had not had the chance of a snowball in hell of winning acquittal. Stovall, Daugherty, and their crew of investigators had gathered evidence and confessions that marked him as a mass killer, and even he could see that.

It was four-fifteen on that warm Friday afternoon when Brudos' plea was entered.

Judge Sloper began with the district attorney. "Mr. Gortmaker?"

"May it please the Court, in the matter of the State of Oregon, plaintiff, versus Jerome Henry Brudos, defendant, case number 67640, the defendant is in court with his attorneys, Mr. Dale Drake and Mr. George Rhoten. This defendant was previously indicted by the Marion County Grand Jury and charged with the crime of murder in the first degree involving

Karen Elena Sprinker allegedly occurring on March 27, 1969. The defendant appeared in court and with his attorneys on the fourth day of June 1969 and entered a plea of not guilty and a plea of not guilty by reason of insanity to the charge alleged in the indictment. I have been informed by the attorneys for the defendant that they desired to appear in court and have a request of the court at this time.

"Also, your Honor, I believe the defendant and his attorneys would like to appear before the court on two other cases, case number 67698, a charge of first-degree murder of Jan Susan Whitney, allegedly occurring on the twenty-sixth day of November 1968; and case number 67700, a charge of first-degree murder of Linda Dawn Salee, allegedly occurring on the twenty-third day of April 1969.

"The defendant appeared in court and with his attorneys on both of these charges and case number 67698 and 67700 on the thirteenth day of June 1969, and entered a plea of not guilty and not guilty by reason of insanity. I believe they have a request of the court in those two cases also."

Judge Sloper turned to Dale Drake. "All right. What is it, Mr. Drake?"

"Yes, your Honor. At this time, the defendant would like to make a motion before the court that he be allowed to withdraw the plea of not guilty by reason of insanity previously entered in case numbers 67640, and 67700, and 67698, the three cases of first-degree murder. The reason for this motion, your Honor, is that subsequent to the entry of said pleas on the dates stated by Mr. Gortmaker previously, the defendant has been examined by the following psychiatrists, all of whom were appointed by the court to examine the defendant. These psychiatrists were Dr. George Suckow, of Oregon state hospital; Drs. Ivor Campbell, Gerhard Haugen, Roger Smith, and Guy Parvaresh, all of Portland, Oregon."

"All right," Sloper said.

"He was examined by Colin Slade and Howard Dewey too, who are two well-known psychologists from Portland. Also, an EEG test was run at the

Oregon state hospital and that was scored by Dr. Phillip Reilly. We have also examined the prior medical histories of the defendant which were present for our examination at the Oregon state hospital when the defendant was incarcerated there in 1956 and 1957.

"Based upon these reports and our own discussions with our client, we are certain at this time that the defendant is able to assist us in his defense. I might say, your Honor, that all of the reports and the examinations and diagnoses by each psychiatrist was substantially the same, and therefore, at this time, we would like to have this report by Dr. Guy Parvaresh marked as Defendant's Exhibit 1, and we would offer it at this time in aid of this motion."

Jerry Brudos sat implacably while the list of doctors who had found him eminently sane was read to the court. At length Judge Sloper asked the defendant himself to rise. Asked if he agreed with Drake's motion to plead guilty, he said that, yes, he had discussed the question with Rhoten and Drake and found that a guilty plea was "the most reasonable approach." He was quite willing to stipulate that he was able to intelligently assist his attorneys.

Indeed, Brudos seemed oddly pleased to be considered so sane and intelligent; it was what he had always wanted people to know.

Drake rose to formally withdraw the not-guilty-by-reason-of-insanity pleas. Sloper listened without expression and then asked, "And what would be the subsequent plea if you are permitted to do so?"

Drake's words dropped like stones in the quiet courtroom. "Guilty, your Honor."

"Mr. Drake, have you and Mr. Rhoten had the opportunity, and have you examined all of the—so far as you are aware—the state's files and the state's evidence?"

Dale Drake explained that he had been available to Jerry Brudos since the Friday night of his arrest—May 30—and that he had been formally appointed to represent Brudos the following Monday morning.

"From Friday night forward, I have been associated with this case, and I have examined the evidence at the time it was taken into custody by the state. Since that time, Mr. Rhoten and myself have examined this morning all of the evidence held by the state, the results of the crime-lab tests, and many pictures and physical evidence of that nature. The state has been most cooperative in this matter."

Sloper turned to the district attorney. "Mr. Gortmaker, have you as a matter of fact disclosed to the defendant's attorneys your complete files and all of the evidence that has been accumulated for the prosecution of these three cases?"

"Yes, your Honor. There was, by Detective Sergeant Stovall of the Salem City Police Department, and Lieutenant Eugene Daugherty of the Oregon state police, assembled at my request all of the exhibits anticipated for trial, together with the statements of witnesses, and a list of anticipated witnesses to be called by the state, and all of this evidence was made available to the defendant's attorneys. They did examine each exhibit, talked to the officers concerning the effect of physical evidence, where it was found and how it was acquired, and so far as I know, all of the evidence we anticipated using in the trial next Monday was made available. . . ."

It is a necessary paradox, inherent in the law, that what begins with such profound emotions as terror and panic must come down to the dry, stolid language of the courtroom. Jerry Brudos' victims had had no chance; he, now, had every chance to understand the ramifications of his guilty pleas.

Did he understand the penalty for conviction of murder in the first degree?

"Yes, your Honor. Life imprisonment."

Sloper wanted to be sure he *really* understood the penalties. It was unlikely that cases so heinous would be punishable at a bargain rate—three for the price of one. "Do you understand that the court has the right in a situation, such as here, where there are multiple charges, that it can direct that the sentence imposed may run consecutively to one earlier imposed, and that it is possible that the maximum penalty in this case could be to sentence you to the Oregon State

Penitentiary for an indeterminate period of time, the maximum of which is your life, three different times, and two of them to run consecutively to the first, and to each other? Are you aware of that?"

"No, your Honor, I wasn't. That's something that didn't come up in the discussion."

"All right, that's good. Would that make a difference to you in expressing a desire to withdraw your plea of not guilty and enter another plea at this time?"

"No, your Honor."

"Has anybody threatened or coerced or intimidated you in any manner at all, in order to coerce you to ask the court's permission to change your plea from not guilty to guilty?"

"No, sir."

"Has anybody promised you anything by way of reward or leniency by the court or anything of that nature to induce you to plead guilty?"

"No, sir."

"Are you aware that under your plea of not guilty, you have a right to require the State of Oregon to establish your guilt to the satisfaction of twelve jurors beyond a reasonable doubt of the truth of the allegations of each of these indictments, or you would be entitled to have the indictments dismissed?"

"Yes, sir."

"Are you also aware that you have a right to remain absolutely silent concerning these charges, and that you cannot be compelled to be a witness in any of the three cases against yourself?"

"Yes, sir."

"And are you also aware of the further right that you have to compel the State to produce here in open court, in the event of a trial, the persons who testified against you, and to face your accuser face to face?"

"Yes, sir."

Judge Sloper picked up a copy of the document entitled "Petition to enter plea of guilty" and went over it paragraph by paragraph with Jerry Brudos. It was the guilty plea in the first case—in the death of Karen Sprinker. It too reduced horror to a few paragraphs, executed in perfect legalese.

Judge Sloper read the third paragraph to Brudos:

"The third paragraph states that, 'I have received a copy of the indictment, being called upon to enter a plea. I am able to read and write and I have read the indictment and I have discussed it with my lawyer. I fully understand every charge made against me. The following is the name of the offense: Murder in the first degree. The elements of the above crime are: That I, Jerome Henry Brudos, on or about the twenty-seventh day of March 1969, in the county of Marion, state of Oregon, purposely and with deliberate and premeditated malice did kill one Karen Elena Sprinker, by strangling and smothering her to death.'"

Judge Sloper asked a few more questions, just to be sure that Jerry Brudos understood what he was pleading guilty to. "Why is that you want to plead guilty to these indictments?"

"Well, your Honor, I did it."

"Now, by your plea of guilty and by your saying, 'I did it,' tell me exactly what it is that you did in connection with this indictment, and one Karen Elena Sprinker."

"I abducted her and strangled her to death."

"Did you do this with a deliberate plan in mind?"

"That I don't honestly have an answer for, your Honor."

"Maybe I could define 'deliberate' a little bit for you. You have told me that you killed Karen Elena Sprinker by strangling her and smothering her, after you had abducted her. How long was she in your company—or custody—before you did the act as alleged in the indictment?"

"About an hour."

"And during that time that she was in your custody, a period of an hour, did you during that period of time make up your mind and plan how you were going to strangle or smother her?" Sloper asked.

"No, sir, there was no plan to strangle or smother her—"

Judge Sloper appeared startled at Brudos' bland denial of what he might have had in his mind during the time he kept Karen Sprinker captive. Sloper's words burst out. "There was no *what*?"

"—no plan to strangle or smother her."

Sloper continued his questions, his voice once again free of emotional emphasis. "How did you do the act?"

"Strangled her with a rope."

"Where had you abducted Miss Sprinker?"

"From the Fred Meyer . . . er . . . the Meier and Frank parking lot."

It continued, the same phrases, the legal rituals to be gone through—only this time for Jan Susan Whitney.

"In connection with indictment number 67698, Mr. Brudos, wherein it is alleged that on the twenty-sixth day of November 1968, in Marion County, Oregon, that you purposely and with deliberate and premeditated malice feloniously killed one Jan Susan Whitney by strangling and smothering said Jan Susan Whitney to death, is it your desire to enter a plea of guilty at this time?"

"Yes, sir."

"And why do you want to plead guilty to this indictment?"

"Because I did do it."

"Can you tell me how you did it?"

"With a leather strap . . . strangled her to death."

"Was this after you had first abducted her?"

"Yes, sir."

"And how long was she in your company or custody before you strangled or smothered her?"

"About twenty minutes."

"How did you strangle or smother her with a leather strap?"

"I had a slipknot on it and I put it around her neck and yanked it tight."

"Was that act, then, deliberate?"

"I really don't know. It just happened."

"In connection with indictment number 67700 . . . you are accused of the crime of first-degree murder of one Linda Dawn Salee. . . . Is it your desire to enter a plea of guilty to that indictment at this time?"

"Yes, sir."

"And why do you want to plead guilty to that indictment?"

"Because I did do it."

"And how did you do that?"

"With a leather strap."

"Perhaps if you would give me a little more detail rather than by saying 'with a leather strap,' I could—"

"I had a leather strap with a knot in it and I just put it around her throat and pulled it tight."

"How long was she in your company or custody before the strangulation?"

"About an hour."

"Did you kill Linda Dawn Salee with deliberation and premeditation?"

"Yes, sir."

Brudos' definite answer the third time this question was posed puzzled Judge Sloper a little. The defendant had waffled on deliberation with Karen and Jan—but then Judge Sloper could not have known how angry Jerry Brudos had been with Linda Salee because she fought him to save her life.

"Is there any difference, so far as your deliberate and premeditated acts are concerned, between Linda Dawn Salee, than there was with Jan Susan Whitney?"

"Pardon?" Brudos was puzzled now.

"Is there any difference in the deliberation or the premeditation that was in your mind at the time you strangled Linda Dawn Salee than there was when you strangled Jan Susan Whitney?"

"No, sir."

"One final question, Mr. Brudos. Are you stating to me at this time, in each of these cases, that you did the acts alleged, with deliberation and with premeditated malice?"

"Yes, sir."

Jerry Brudos had now pleaded guilty to killing Karen and Jan and Linda Salee (charges in the death of Linda Slawson, if initiated, would have to come from another jurisdiction, Multnomah County). The confessed killer had the right by law to have sentencing delayed for forty-eight hours. He asked that the waiting period be waived and that his sentence be read immediately.

Three months—to the day—had passed since Jerry Brudos had seized Karen Sprinker in the store parking lot. Starting with no clues at all, Jim Stovall and Gene Daugherty—the whole investigation team—had found the killer, arrested him, and now saw him sentenced for his crimes, the near-impossible accomplished in ninety days.

"Jerome Henry Brudos, in case number 67640, in which you have pled guilty to the first-degree murder of Karen Elena Sprinker, it is the judgment of this Court that you be committed to the custody of the Corrections Division of the Oregon State Board of Control for an indeterminate period of time, the maximum of which is the balance of your natural life.

"In connection with case number 67698, in which you have entered a plea of guilty to first-degree murder in the death of one Jan Susan Whitney, it is the judgment of the Court that you be committed to the custody of the Corrections Division of the Oregon State Board of Control for an indeterminate period of time, the maximum of which shall be the balance of your natural life. It will be the further order of the Court that the sentence shall run consecutively to the sentence just previously imposed in case number 67640."

One more.

"In connection with indictment number 67700, the indictment to which you have just entered a plea of guilty to first-degree murder of one Linda Dawn Salee, it will be the judgment of the Court that you be committed to the custody of the Corrections Division of the Oregon State Board of Control for an indeterminate period of time, the maximum of which is the balance of your natural life. This sentence shall run consecutively to the sentences just imposed in cases numbered 67698 and 67640.

"That will be all. You are remanded to the custody of the warden of the Oregon State Penitentiary.

"Court will be in recess."

*   *   *

It seemed to be over. The expected circus of horror in the courtroom stopped before it began. Jerome Henry Brudos had three life sentences. Of course, "life" does not mean *life*, actual life, when it is a word in a prison sentence. With good behavior, a lifer in Oregon can expect to be out in about twelve years. Jerry Brudos worked, however, under the burden of *three* consecutive life sentences. If he were to serve them all—even with good-behavior credits—he could not hope to be free for thirty-six years. He would be sixty-six years old at least if, and when, he ever got out.

Brudos had a new address: 2605 State Street—the Oregon State Penitentiary. He had become Number 33284.

He thought a lot about his situation, and the more he thought about it, the more unfair it seemed.

Hell, it had always been that way. People pushed him around and took advantage of him. It wasn't fair.

It wasn't fair at all.

— 21 —

Darcie Brudos still lived with her cousin; she was dependent on her relatives financially and embarrassed about it. Her husband was in prison—apparently forever—and that seemed to be the only way it could have ended. Her children remained with her parents, and what possessions she still owned were scattered, some of them in police custody.

On July 1, Darcie Brudos did something she had sworn she would never do: she applied for welfare. She was found to be eligible immediately for an aid-to-dependent-children grant, and Darcie and the youngsters set up a home again. She attempted to look at the future with some optimism, but it was heavy work to do so. Her life—since she had met Jerry—seemed to have progressed in a steady series of descending steps. When she had thought that things could not get worse, they always *had* gotten worse. It was something of a relief for her to know that Jerry was in prison. She believed now that he had done what they had accused him of, but she still could not dwell on it.

It made her too frightened.

Jerry's surprise guilty pleas had caught the press off guard, and they had reacted out of some frustration—printing every detail they could ferret out. Everybody seemed to know about him and about what he had done. She knew that she would divorce him as soon as she could, and that she would change her name—perhaps even move far away where no one had ever heard of Jerry Brudos.

But not right away. The children were too upset, and she had no confidence that she could make a life for them away from her family.

Hers was the common plight of a woman who has never been without a man to tell her what to do. Certainly she had chafed under the restrictions of her father and then her husband, but she had never had the fortitude to defy either of them. Alone now, she moved through her days tentatively. When she was strong enough, she would get a job, and then the divorce, and then the name change. . . .

If Darcie Brudos felt disbelief and shock, so did the public. Armed with the printed details of Jerry Brudos' crimes that had been gleaned by the somewhat disappointed media, bereft of the expected trial, the public had a field day whispering about Darcie Brudos. It seemed inconceivable that any woman could be so submissive and unaware that her husband could have carried on a series of killings in their own home without her knowledge. The rumormongers were busy.

The general consensus of the public was that Jerry and Darcie Brudos had surely engaged in kinky sex—sex that eventually demanded the presence of other women to fulfill their bizarre scenarios. After all, breast molds and women's underwear had been discovered right in the Brudos home. What woman could have ignored those items? What decent woman would have put up with it without asking questions?

The words and insinuations became almost palpable entities, and rumors and tips flooded the Salem Police Department and the Oregon Children's Protection offices.

The public had not had its full revenge on Jerry Brudos; he had pleaded guilty without a trial, and he had somehow robbed the public. There was the prevailing feeling that the whole story had not been revealed, that something was being held back.

Jim Stovall had never felt that Darcie Brudos had any guilty knowledge of her husband's crimes. He had talked to the man for days, and he had seen a kind of gentleness in Brudos toward his wife—an almost protective sense. The man *was* devious and cruel, but he had also seemed to hold Darcie, however neurotically, above the rest of the world. Stovall doubted that she could have played any part at all in the acting out of her husband's fantasies. His impression of Darcie was that she was truly naive, frightened . . . and innocent.

He had seen, of course, the nude photos of Darcie that Jerry had kept—and he saw that she appeared to wear the same black patent-leather shoes that Karen Sprinker had worn in her last pictures. He did not believe that indicated she had guilty knowledge.

Others did not agree with him.

Mrs. Edna Beecham was convinced that she had important information to tell the police. The more she thought about it, the more she knew she must go to someone and tell her story.

Edna Beecham's sister lived in the house that abutted the Brudos garage, and Mrs. Beecham visited her sister often. She had occasionally had coffee with Darcie Brudos—and she'd liked her well enough. Then.

But Edna Beecham became convinced she had seen something on the afternoon of March 27. It became quite clear in her mind. She talked it over with her sister, and she talked about it with other friends, and they all urged her to go to the police.

And she did.

"I saw something," she began. "I saw something on the afternoon of March 27—about one-thirty P.M. I have to tell . . ."

Life was going to continue to get worse for Darcie Brudos.

On July 17, Jim Stovall and Detective B. J. Miller, accompanied by Salem police Detective Marilyn Dezsofi, drove to Corvallis. Their destination was the home of Darcie Brudos' parents; the grandparents had had custody of Megan, now seven, and Jason, twenty-three months old for several weeks. Now the youngsters were to be placed, at least temporarily, under the custody of the Oregon State Childrens' Services Division.

Jim Stovall carried Jason to the car and Megan took Marilyn Dezsofi's hand. It was a sad errand for the detectives, but necessary. Darcie Brudos had now become the focal point of an ongoing investigation.

Megan Brudos was a smart little girl, and Dezsofi was astounded when the child commented matter-of-factly, "My daddy killed three . . . I mean, five women."

Dezsofi, Miller, and Stovall said nothing, and Megan continued to chatter. "I don't like policemen very well—they came and got my Daddy and put him in that place. Are you policemen?"

Dezsofi nodded.

"Was that man one of them that got my daddy?" she asked, pointing to Jim Stovall. Stovall nodded slightly.

Apparently, conversation about the case had not been soft-pedaled around Megan by her mother and grandparents. "My daddy's sick in the head," Megan confided. "He was sick in the head when he was a little boy and he got sicker and now he is so sick, he will never get well. My mom says we're going to have to change our last name."

Megan babbled quite freely to Dezsofi on the way to a foster home in Jefferson. "You know, my brother is too young to know what Daddy did!"

The little girl said that she knew many secrets, and she might tell them later.

But she didn't. The next time the detectives talked with her she blurted, "I forgot all my secrets."

It would always be questionable how much Megan truly knew, and how much of her knowledge had come from overhearing bits and pieces of conversation. She did not recognize pictures of any of the victims, and she laughed out loud when Dezsofi asked her if her father ever put on ladies' shoes for fun.

"Daddy wear women's shoes?" she chortled, as if the idea was absolutely ridiculous.

In the end, Jim Stovall was convinced that Megan had no valuable information. Further, he didn't want to subject the youngster to detailed questioning on matters concerning her father's crimes. Her life would be difficult enough from here on.

Darcie Brudos was stunned almost to inaction when her children were placed in foster care, and she asked Salem attorneys Charles Burt and Richard Seideman to represent her. She was not sure why her children had been taken from her.

Early on the morning of August 7, the reason was quite clear. Richard Seideman called Darcie and told her that she was being charged with first-degree murder, *i.e.*, aiding and abetting Jerome Brudos in the murder of Karen Sprinker. "You will be arraigned in half an hour."

The wait was not half an hour, but four hours long, and Darcie left the arraignment to walk the gauntlet past the strobe lights of cameras. Reporters described her in print later as "emotionless," "calm," and "stolid." In reality, she had been too numb to react. She moved through her weeks in jail in a kind of dream. *This* was the worst thing, the thing that had been waiting for her all along . . . but something she had never dreamed in her worst nightmares might happen.

The burden of the state was predictable. To prove that Darcie Brudos was guilty of aiding and abetting her husband in the death of Karen Sprinker, the case against Brudos himself must be presented. All the evidence would have to be brought out, all the ugliness paraded before a jury. Whatever the final verdict, the decision would be something of a legal landmark.

It began—this final ordeal—in September 1969.

Since he had presided over Jerry Brudos' hearings, Judge Sloper disqualified himself and Judge Hay would preside. The opposing attorneys were well-matched, perhaps the most outstanding criminal lawyers in Marion County. For the state, Gary D. Gortmaker, tall, confident, his prematurely silver hair perfectly cut—an almost constant winner in court. For the defense, Charlie Burt. Burt is a man of short stature, slightly crippled by a childhood bout with polio, somewhat irascible, gruffness hiding his innate kindness. Both men were in their early forties.

The courtroom had 125 seats for spectators, and there were hundreds of would-be observers waiting outside the locked doors each morning, all vying for a seat. Spectators' purses and packages were searched before they were allowed into the courtroom; threats against Darcie Brudos' life had been voiced.

Those who were lucky enough to get a seat would not budge, even during recesses. They watched Darcie Brudos, and commented in stage whispers that she did not "look like a murderess." She did not; in her white blouse and neat dark suit, her short hair tousled, she looked very young and very frightened. She was much thinner than she was when Jerry was arrested. The pounds she'd fought for years had slid away with the tension of the past four months.

She was only twenty-four, a very young twenty-four. She could hear them talking behind her. She heard muffled laughter and a constant undertone of conversation, as if the gallery believed she could not hear their comments.

"If anybody dies, just prop him up—and keep your seat. We don't want to miss anything."

She saw a hugely pregnant woman who seemed about ready to deliver, and thought how uncomfortable she must be sitting all day on a hard courtroom bench. And then the woman said, "I hope I have the baby over the weekend so I can be back here by Monday morning. . . ."

She saw the armed deputies leaning against the back wall, and realized with a shock that they were there to protect *her* from the possibility of attack by someone who had already judged her and found her guilty.

The first panel of prospective jurors—forty in all— was exhausted by noon of the first day of jury selection; they had all read about the "Brudos case," and they had all formed opinions as to her guilt or innocence. It would take two and a half days to select a jury. Eight women and four men. And then she wondered. It was such a toss-up. She knew women could judge another woman far more harshly than men did. Would they understand? Would they believe her?

It was time to begin. District Attorney Gortmaker rose to make his opening remarks to the jury. Gortmaker assured the jury that he would prove that Darcie Brudos had helped her husband when he'd killed Karen Sprinker. He said he would produce an eyewitness who had *seen* Darcie assist Brudos in forcing a person wrapped in a blanket into their home. . . .

Charlie Burt spoke next. He stressed that Darcie had had no reason at all to aid her husband. He pointed out that Darcie had refused to destroy evidence, had actually saved physical evidence for the police to find. "This is hardly the act of a woman trying to protect herself!"

On the first morning of the trial, Megan Brudos was called into the courtroom so that Judge Hay could determine if she would be a competent witness. A witness against her mother. . . . Darcie had not seen her daughter for over two months. Seeing Megan walk timidly into the courtroom was almost more than she could bear. Megan was only seven years old; she seemed so frail, thinner than she had been, and quite frightened.

The testimony of a child under ten in a court of law is always suspect. Some children are mature enough to relate facts accurately; others are not. Judge Hay leaned toward Megan and smiled as he spoke softly to her.

"What is your name?"

"Megan."

"What do you think happens when you don't tell the truth?"

"You get in trouble."

"Do you believe in God?"

"Yes."

"How are your marks in school?"

"I got some bad marks . . ."

"But some good ones too?"

"Yes, they balance out."

"Do you think you could answer questions honestly—if someone should ask you in this courtroom?"

"Yes."

Both the defense and prosecution declined to question Megan at this time. The child looked around the courtroom for the first time, and she saw her mother. She began to cry.

And so did Darcie.

Megan was led from the room—but she had been accepted as a potential witness against her mother.

On Thursday morning, September 25, the prosecution's case began in earnest. Lieutenant Robert W.

Pinnick of the state crime lab took the stand to identify clothing removed from Karen Sprinker's body.

"Were there articles of clothing that you removed
from the body of the deceased?" Gortmaker asked.

"I removed from the badly decomposed body of
Karen Sprinker . . . white panties, a black long-line
bra, a green skirt . . . a green sweater."

The courtroom was very quiet as Pinnick broke the
seal on the bags holding the clothing, and there was a
concurrent odor that insinuated itself into the close
air. (When Darcie Brudos' trial was over, the courtroom would retain the stench, a stench removed only
by having all the benches stripped and revarnished.)

Each garment was displayed after Pinnick identified
his own initials on the labels of the bags that held them.

"Did you find anything inside the strapless brassiere?"

"Yes, sir."

"What was that?"

"Brown—or tan—paper towels had been stuffed into
the cups."

"When the body was examined—on autopsy—were
the breasts intact?"

"They were not. They were absent."

There was no carnival atmosphere now. There were
only shocked gasps, and Darcie felt the force of eyes
staring behind her.

She had not known. This she had not known.

Burt and Seideman had tried to warn Darcie what
the physical evidence would be like; she had listened
and nodded, but she had not foreseen how awful it
really was. The defense team had tried to keep the
evidence out of trial, but all two thousand pieces of it
were allowed, trundled into the courtroom by deputies
before each session.

Lieutenant Pinnick described the manner in which
Karen Sprinker's body was weighted down with an
engine head from a Chevrolet, the mass of it attached
with nylon rope—microscopically identical in class and
characteristic with the nylon rope taken from Jerry
Brudos' workshop.

"Did you form an opinion on whether the victim
had been undressed . . . or redressed?"

"Yes, sir. She apparently had been. The black brassiere was not hers."

"Did you go to 3123 Center Street on June 3, 1969, to participate in a search of the premises?"

"Yes, sir."

"And did you seize certain items of evidentiary value from those premises?"

"Yes, sir."

Darcie watched as piece after piece of evidence was introduced, identified by Pinnick, and accepted. Here in the courtroom, it all seemed to have a macabre air—although some of the items were quite familiar to her: the blue shag rug (that Jerry had said he needed to keep his feet warm in the workshop), his tool chest, the vise, a gas can, a green plastic wastebasket, a reloading device for ammunition, his rock tumbler, a blue wooden box and a gray metal kitchen stool. She had seen all those things on the rare occasion that he allowed her into the workshop. She was not sure what they might possibly have to do with his crimes.

For the rest of the day, the morass of evidence grew, and as it grew, Darcie began to feel physically ill.

There were the shoes—she had seen none of them. The women's low shoes with laces she had never seen before. Were they Karen Sprinker's? The prosecution said they had been. And all of the others. Where had he gotten them, and how had he kept them so secret from her?

All the things the police had found in the attic. Gortmaker lifted packages from a huge box, packages to be opened to show that they contained so many brassieres . . . and girdles. Jerry had obviously stolen these things, and she had had no idea.

Her attorneys had warned Darcie that there would be terrible pictures, and now they were handed to Lieutenant Pinnick for identification, passed to the defense table for Darcie's perusal, and then given to the jury. She was afraid she was going to vomit.

She saw the hanging body of a woman who hung as still as death from a hook in Jerry's workshop, her face covered with a black hood. The next girl, who had to be Karen Sprinker—she recognized her face from newspaper stories—gazed into the camera with an awful kind of fear in her eyes. She wore only panties and shiny black pumps, and she stood on Jerry's blue rug. . . .

There was a black notebook—she had never seen it before—and it held pages of pictures of naked female torsos. The women photographed had no heads; they had been snipped from the photos. Why? To avoid identification? Or as a symbolic gesture of violence? Darcie studied the headless nude photos and wondered who they were—or who they had been.

There were pictures of Jerry. Jerry dressed grotesquely in women's underclothing—wearing a black slip, stockings, and high heels. She had seen him like this, but she had put it out of her mind.

And then the worst picture of all. The dead girl hanging from the ceiling by the rope around her neck. And Jerry. Her husband's face was there, too; he had leaned too far over the mirror on the floor, photographing himself along with the dead woman when he snapped this terrible picture.

Darcie looked up at the jury and saw that their faces were gray and sickened as they passed the pictures down the line. She saw a woman look at one of the pictures, shut her eyes against the image, and swallow hard.

What else would they show? Darcie knew she was living in a nightmare now. How could she have been in the same house with Jerry and not have realized how sick he was? How could she convince anyone that she had not known?

She opened her eyes and saw that Lieutenant Pinnick was holding up the breast paperweight that Jerry had explained away so blithely. Now she could see it for what it was. A life model of a full female breast, almost five inches across.

"Where was this mold located?" District Attorney Gortmaker asked.

"In the home."

"*In* the home?"

"Yes, sir. It was on a shelf above the fireplace."

Darcie felt the jurors' eyes turn toward her. She

knew they were wondering how she could have avoided seeing this exhibit. She bent her head toward the yellow legal pad Mr. Burt had given her. He had told her she could take notes if she liked—but it was really only something to do with her hands when she could no longer bear the stares and whispers.

When the long day in court was finally over, the clerk's desk was piled with the evidence. Not against Jerry—not really now—because Jerry was in prison.

She was the one on trial.

Darcie Brudos had seen Edna Beecham's name on the state's witness list, and she'd been confused by it. She could not imagine what Edna Beecham might have to say. Edna Beecham was a friend, although not a close friend. Just a talkative, slightly gossipy woman who'd been pleasant over coffee.

Edna Beecham would not look at her now; she seemed too eager to plunge into her testimony. So eager, in fact, that Judge Hay had to caution the witness to slow down and tell only those things that were responsive to the questions Gortmaker posed to her.

"Please tell the jury what you remember of March 27, 1969."

"I was at my sister's house that day."

"Can you point out on the map behind you where your sister's home is located, please."

Edna Beecham took the pointer and indicated a house whose yard touched the Brudos garage.

"Mark it with an X if you will, Mrs. Beecham."

Darcie waited while Edna Beecham made a careful cross on the map and then took her seat again.

"What time was it that you were visiting your sister?"

"All day. I was visiting from over in Bend. I was looking out the dining-room window about one-thirty P.M. I saw Mr. Brudos. He was pushing something—someone—with a blanket around them from the garage toward the kitchen door. The kitchen door was open. There were three cement steps that went up to the porch . . . it's a kind of cement platform there. Mrs. Brudos was standing there on the porch part . . ."

Darcie's mouth fell open in shock, and she turned to whisper to Mr. Burt, but he only shook his head slightly. Mrs. Beecham was still talking.

". . . The girl tried to jerk away. But Mrs. Brudos helped Mr. Brudos push the person in the blanket into the house."

Edna Beecham spoke with conviction. She had seen what she had seen, and she seemed anxious to tell it all. She was adamant that she had seen the Brudoses—both of them—struggling to get the blanket-wrapped form into their house.

It was finally time for cross-examination from the defense. Charlie Burt rose easily and walked toward Mrs. Beecham with a disarming smile. She smiled back nervously.

"Mrs. Beecham . . . you say that you saw Mr. Brudos push someone from the garage to the kitchen door?"

"Yes." She got up from her witness chair and demonstrated. "She was pushed up against Mr. Brudos' chest. He had his arms around the girl's body in front. The girl had a gag in her mouth—"

"Oh? She had an adhesive-tape gag?"

"I didn't say adhesive tape—"

"If she had—as you said—a blanket over her head, how could you see the gag?"

"There was an opening there. I saw the gag."

"What color was the blanket?"

"I don't know."

"Are you color blind?"

"No . . . but I don't know. The blanket had a binding on it."

"What color was the binding?"

"I don't know."

"The binding is stitching around the edge?"

"No . . . no, it's material."

"How do you know the blanket-covered figure was a girl?"

"I could tell by the outline. I could see the legs and the shoes."

"What color were the shoes?"

"I don't know."

"Were they red?"

"I do not know. I do know her nylons were cocoa beige."

Sound rippled through the gallery; the woman's memory was oddly selective.

"What was Mr. Brudos wearing?"

"I don't know."

"How is it, Mrs. Beecham, that you could see the Brudos home so clearly, given that there is a tall evergreen hedge between that property and your sister's property?"

The witness had been fingering a rosary in her lap throughout her testimony. Now she threw up her left hand dramatically and cried, "As God is above, I *saw* it!"

"Mrs. Beecham," Burt said quietly. "If you saw Mr. Brudos, assisted by Mrs. Brudos—saw them forcing a young woman with . . . cocoa-beige stockings, and wrapped in a blanket whose color you can not now recall—if you saw them forcing her into their home, why didn't you call the police?"

"My sister asked me not to."

"I see. Your sister asked you not to. Did you tell anyone else?"

"My husband."

Burt allowed Mrs. Beecham's time lapse in calling the police to sink into the jury's minds before he gathered photographs of views of the Brudos home taken from the witness's sister's home.

"These pictures were taken from your sister's dining-room window," he said. "This doesn't appear to be a good vantage point."

Mrs. Beecham studied the pictures and looked up. "This picture doesn't look right to me."

"Wasn't there something that cut your view of the Brudos house off—something in the way?"

"Nothing cut my view. I was up high. Yes, there was this cedar hedge and trees—but I saw everything."

"Did you see the back door of the Brudos home?"

"I'm getting mixed up about the door," she answered. "I could see the cement platform—I couldn't see the kitchen door."

"How about in this angle," Burt asked, handing her another picture taken from her sister's home.

Mrs. Beecham grew more confident. "Branches were not on the trees—I mean, leaves—and I saw the door close. I just don't know much about trees."

"Do you know that evergreen trees—such as cedar—do not lose their leaves?"

"Yes," she said shortly. "I know that much."

"But you say you saw the incident clearly *through* the cedar hedge?"

"I saw it."

"When did you reconstruct your . . . view for the Salem police?"

"Last month."

Jim Stovall listened to Edna Beecham on the stand, just as he had listened to her when he had traveled to Bend, Oregon, at the request of the district attorney's office. Her story had not entirely convinced him then, and it didn't now. "But," he recalls, "when you testify before a grand jury, nobody asks your own opinion; they only ask about what witnesses told you."

Burt's cross-examination of Edna Beecham had shown the woman's confusion and pointed out that she had done nothing whatsoever after allegedly seeing something that demanded action. She simply could not have seen what she said she had.

Darcie felt slightly better.

But she felt worse again when the next prosecution witness was called: Megan Brudos.

Megan entered the courtroom slowly, a tiny figure all dressed in blue with her coat over her arm. She seemed on the edge of tears, but she walked bravely to the witness stand.

She looked up at District Attorney Gortmaker and waited for him to question her. He asked her name again, asked a few casual questions to help her relax, and then he began the hard questions.

"Megan, did your mommy and daddy tell you not to tell anybody what happened in the workshop?"

"I . . . can't remember."

"Did you hear crying coming from the workshop a couple of times that day—that day last March?"

"I can't remember."

"Did you meet a girl about the time of spring vacation named Karen that your daddy took into the workshop while your mother was home?"

"*Yes.*"

The courtroom buzzed again, and Darcie shook her head slightly.

"While Karen was there, did your mother go into the workshop and start crying—and then come out of the workshop and go into the bedroom and lie on the bed and cry?"

"I can't remember."

Darcie had cried so many times over the past months. She had tried not to, tried not to let the children know how desperate and sad she felt. Megan had seen her cry. But Megan could never have seen her cry under the circumstances Gortmaker had described.

"Isn't it true, Megan," the district attorney continued, "that Mommy didn't like to help Daddy when the girls were in the workshop because your daddy wanted to take pictures of them and your mommy didn't want him to?"

"I don't know."

Gortmaker gave it up. As a witness for the prosecution, Megan Brudos had emerged, instead, as a very sad, very confused little girl.

Charlie Burt asked only two questions on cross-examination.

"Megan, did Sergeant Stovall show you some pictures of girls—big girls—and did he ask you if you knew any of them, if you recognized them?"

"Yes."

"The girl we're asking about, the girl named Karen, was in those pictures. Did you tell Sergeant Stovall that you had seen her?"

"No. By the looks of them, I didn't know anyone in those pictures."

The prosecution's presentation was over finally, and it was Charlie Burt's turn to attempt to prove to the jury that Darcie Brudos was in no way connected to her husband's crimes.

Her brother-in-law, Larry, was asked to describe

Jerry Brudos' character. "He is aggressive . . . over-bearing to the point of violence—at least to me and to our parents."

"Who was the dominant partner in the marriage of your brother and Darcie Brudos?" Burt asked.

"I don't think there's any doubt about that. My brother was."

Ned Rawls told the jury of Jerry Brudos' sheer physical strength. He told of Jerry Brudos lifting engine heads and other heavy automobile parts with ease.

"Did Jerry Brudos show you anything when you visited his home on the twenty-ninth of March this year?"

"He showed me photographs of women—nude women's figures."

"What did the women look like?"

"I couldn't tell you. The faces had been snipped out of the photos."

"Did you see anything else on that night that seemed a little strange to you?"

"The breast molds. Lead or something shaped like a woman's breast. He said a friend had asked him to make a paperweight shaped like a breast."

"Did he say who the friend was?"

"No, sir."

Ned Rawls's wife, Lois, was the next witness.

"Mrs. Rawls," Burt asked, "did you have a conversation with Mrs. Edna Beecham in the corridor outside the grand-jury hearing room this past month?"

"Yes, sir."

"What did she say to you?"

"She said she'd seen Jerry and Darcie with a woman with long dark hair who had a blanket wrapped around her. She said they were pushing her on the back porch."

"Did she tell you how she could see the woman's long dark hair when she had a blanket over her head?"

"No, she didn't."

Darcie Brudos' girlfriends Sherrie, Doris, and Ginny Barron—all sisters-in-law—testified that during the months of February and March 1969 Darcie had spent at least four days a week in their homes, from early morning until just before supper. During that period,

Jerry Brudos had telephoned frequently to check on Darcie's whereabouts.

"She was never allowed to go home without calling him first," Sherrie Barron testified. "She couldn't just walk in on him."

None of them, however, was prepared to swear that Darcie had been with them all day on March 27. It had been a weekday, like any other weekday. There had been no reason at the time to mark it as special.

Charlie Burt called a surprise witness: Dr. Ivor Campbell, one of the psychiatrists who had examined Jerry Brudos. He had also spent hours interviewing Darcie Brudos.

Dr. Campbell characterized Darcie Brudos as essentially a normal woman, hardly a dangerous person—and highly unlikely to be motivated to kill another human being.

"Would it, then, Dr. Campbell," Burt asked, "be easy for someone like Jerry Brudos to dominate the defendant—to push her around and make her afraid to even come into her own home without permission?"

"It would."

"How many times have you testified in court, Dr. Campbell?"

"I would say perhaps sixty-five hundred times."

"You examined Jerome Henry Brudos?"

"I did."

"How would you compare Jerry Brudos to other individuals—patients—you may have testified about?"

"I could not."

"You could *not*?"

"No, sir."

"Why is that?"

"My examination of Jerome Brudos indicated a subject whose mental disturbances were so bizarre . . . *so* bizarre that a psychiatrist might just possibly expect to see one personality like his in an entire lifetime of practice."

"One in a lifetime . . . ?"

"And perhaps not then."

— 22 —

In television productions of murder trials, the accused invariably takes the witness stand in his own defense. In life, it is the exception rather than the rule. If a defendant testifies, he is automatically vulnerable to cross-examination by the prosecution. Most defense attorneys choose not to give the state that opportunity. Tactically, the choice involved in putting the defendant on the stand is something of a toss-up. If the defendant does not testify, there is sometimes the feeling that he has something to hide. A jury may deduce that silence is an admission of guilt. If a defendant has a prior record of offenses, these can be elicited during cross-examination. But Darcie Brudos had no record at all. Charlie Burt chose to have Darcie testify. It was the best way he could demonstrate her personality—this frightened, passive small woman who had convinced him that she was totally innocent.

The courtroom was packed on Thursday, September 30; the word was that *she* would be on the stand, and everyone wanted to hear what she had to say for herself.

Darcie had agreed to testify, just as she had earlier agreed to go for broke—refusing to plead guilty to lesser charges. She was innocent, and she had chosen to risk a guilty verdict rather than live the rest of her life with a cloud of suspicion around her.

Guilt by association has marred the lives of many women who loved evil men. Darcie studied the women on the jury and wondered if they knew *everything* about the men in their lives. Would they believe that men could have secret lives, dark sides of themselves that their women might never imagine? It was an unsettling thought, a thought most women would reject.

For the first time now, she faced the gallery. She knew the questions would be intimate. She would have to tell this sea of strangers about things that she had discussed with no one else—ever.

Charlie Burt smiled at her, and she trusted him. If anyone could help her, he could.

"Darcie, did you have anything to do with bringing anyone into your home on March 27, 1969?"

"No."

"Did you ever have anything to do with aiding your husband in killing anyone?"

"No."

"How long had you known your husband when you married him?"

"Three months."

"What kind of marriage was it in the beginning?"

She could sense the gallery listening. This would be the "good stuff"—a soap opera right before their eyes. "I considered it a very good marriage—at first."

"How long were you married before trouble developed?"

"Three or four years."

"What caused the trouble?"

"There were a lot of things. He wasn't working all the time and we seemed to quarrel about so many things."

"Going back to the time you lived in Salem, how were you getting along?"

"Not very good."

"How much did you stay home?"

"Not very often. I didn't enjoy being home when my husband was there."

"What was causing the quarrels with your husband?"

"Different things he wanted me to do . . . and his not working."

"Were there times he would be sick?"

"Several times he would have what he called migraine headaches. He couldn't stand much noise. The headaches put him in a very bad mood."

"You say you quarreled about things he wanted you

to do. Could you tell us what some of those things were?"

She knew that she had to tell it all. Mr. Burt had explained that the prosecution would bring all those embarrassing things out—that her own lawyer could defuse the impact if he asked her first. "I . . . I objected to having Jerry take pictures of me . . . when I was naked."

Darcie heard a buzzing in the courtroom, a few muffled gasps of disapproval.

"Why did you go along with this . . . this picture-taking?"

"He was my husband. He developed his own film and he said he would destroy the pictures after he finished with them."

"Were there other things you argued about?"

"He wanted me to wear high heels all the time. I have back problems, and it was very uncomfortable for me to do that."

"Did you ever see your husband wearing women's clothing?"

"Yes."

"Could you tell us about that?"

"I was . . . kidding him about being overweight. He went into another room, and when he came back he was wearing a girdle and a brassiere and he asked me if he looked thinner."

Darcie looked down at her hands, and the way Jerry had looked in that outfit flashed back across her mind.

"Did you think it was a joke?"

"Yes."

"Did you have any feelings about your husband's mental condition—that maybe something might be wrong?"

"Yes. Just a feeling—but I'd felt something was wrong for the past few years."

"Did you suspect your husband of killing anyone?" Burt asked bluntly.

"No! No, I did not."

"Darcie, can you tell the jury a little of what your home life was like—during the time you were living in Salem?"

"Yes. I—"

"Were you afraid of your husband?"

"He was—is—very large, and he's very, very strong. He kind of dominated everything that went on. He had rules . . ."

"Rules? For instance . . ."

"I was not allowed to go out to Jerry's workshop in the garage. The freezer was out there. I was not allowed to go out to get food from the freezer. If I wanted something for dinner, I had to call Jerry on the intercom and tell him to bring it in. He explained that he had all kinds of photographic equipment out there and I might ruin his pictures if I came into the workshop without warning him."

"When you were away, where did you go?"

"I went to my friends' homes—to the Barrons' houses."

"What happened when you wanted to come home?"

"I had to call my husband and tell him I was on the way."

"Why was that?"

"I don't know. I was just supposed to call. He called my friends too, to see where I was—to check and see if I was with them."

"Did you ever ask him why he did this?"

"Yes, once I did."

"What did he say?"

"He kind of laughed, and he said he wanted to be sure that he got the blonde out of the house before I got home."

There was a sharp gasp in the courtroom. It was too close to the truth.

"Did you think he was joking?"

"Yes, I did."

"Darcie, do you remember finding pictures of women—nude women—in your husband's workshop?"

"Yes. I went out to do the laundry—I had permission—and I asked my husband about some pictures that I saw in a developing tray. He said they weren't his—that they belonged to some college kid he was doing a favor for."

"Do you remember seeing a breast mold?"

"Yes."

"Did you ask your husband what it was?"

"Yes. He said he was making a paperweight."

"Did you believe him?"

"Yes. I had no reason not to."

"Did you ever find other pictures—pictures of your husband wearing women's clothing?"

"Yes."

"Did you take those pictures? Did you ever take pictures of your husband when he was dressed like that?"

"No I did not."

"Do you know whether he had a camera that could be set to take a photo of himself?"

"He had a thirty-five-millimeter he got in Korea, or from Korea."

"Did you ever see him use it?"

"He took a picture of all of us—Jerry, my son, my daughter, and me—by a 'Leaving California' sign once."

"Darcie," Burt said, "did you receive a phone call from your husband on the night he was arrested—on May 30?"

"Yes, he called me from the jail."

"What did he want you to do?"

"He asked me to go out to his workshop and destroy a box of photographs and a box of women's clothing I'd find there."

"Did you?"

"No, sir. I called Mr. Drake, instead. He told me that it would be illegal for me to destroy something that might be evidence."

"What did you do with those things?"

"The police came in and took them later."

"Did you ever go into the attic of your home?"

"No, sir."

"Why was that?"

"Jerry said there were mice . . . and things like that up there. I'm terrified of mice."

"Darcie Brudos . . . if you suspected that people were being killed in your home, what would you have done?"

"I would have moved out . . . I would have left him."

"How do you feel about your husband now?"

"I feel he is a very sick person. I'm afraid to be with him . . . alone."

Darcie Brudos would now have to establish some manner of alibi for her time on the twenty-seventh of March. For the average person, recall of events on what has seemed to be an ordinary day some months previous is a difficult—if not impossible—task. Businesses keep calendars; housewives seldom do. How can one remember what happened on a weekday? Darcie had gone over her days again and again, and she had narrowed down her activities on that Thursday, only because the day had been somewhat unusual. She followed Charlie Burt's instructions to relate what she remembered of the twenty-seventh to the jury.

"That day was a Thursday. I had been at Ginny Barron's from about nine or nine-thirty. I had planned to stay all day, but Jerry called about two and suggested that we drive to Corvallis to see my parents. I went home, and I think we left for Corvallis about three. But when we got to my parents', Jerry just dropped us off and said he had to see friends and would be back for supper. He didn't come back for supper at all. I remember that because my mother had fixed extra food for him, and he didn't even come or call to say he'd be late. He finally showed up around nine—and he had one of his bad migraine headaches."

If Darcie Brudos was telling the truth about that last day of Karen Sprinker's life, it appeared that Jerry Brudos had arranged to have his family far away from their home while he violated his victim's body. Only later, long after midnight, had he secreted the body in his station wagon and driven back to the Long Tom to dispose of it.

On cross-examination, District Attorney Gortmaker questioned the defendant closely about the cameras the family had owned. There had been several—two movie cameras and three still cameras. The delayed-timing mechanism had not been found in Brudos' workshop, and Gortmaker suggested that Darcie—and not Jerry—had taken the gruesome picture of Karen's body which showed Brudos' face.

Darcie had no idea how the delayed-timing mechanism worked. But she was firm in her response to suggestions that she had been the person behind the camera when those terrible pictures were taken.

Gortmaker picked up some glossy eight-by-tens of different pairs of shoes, including the black patent-leather pumps.

"Mrs. Brudos, can you identify these shoes? Are they yours?"

"No."

It was over—for the moment. Darcie Brudos left the witness stand.

Charlie Burt called her parents to the stand. They were quite sure of the date that Jerry Brudos had driven his family to Corvallis. They could not swear to it.

The next defense witness was Harry Nordstrom, a man who said he had known Edna Beecham for seventeen years.

"Mr. Nordstrom," Burt asked, "were you ever in a position to hear a conversation between Mrs. Beecham and her sister—a conversation regarding something Mrs. Beecham had seen from her sister's dining-room window?"

"Yes, sir. On two occasions."

"What did Mrs. Beecham say?"

"She was trying to convince her sister that she had seen Jerry Brudos force a struggling girl into their home—the Brudos home."

"How did she say that was accomplished?"

"One time she said that Jerry carried the girl in—and once she said she saw him lead her in."

"Carried?"

"Yes."

"And the next time, she had changed her recall. She said *led* in?"

"Yes, sir."

"Mr. Nordstrom, based on your acquaintance with Mrs. Beecham—for seventeen years—how would you estimate Mrs. Beecham's reputation for telling the truth?"

Nordstrom paused, and then he answered softly. "She tells the truth . . . as she knows it."

Burt had pretty well eliminated the state's prize witness as credible. He still had to attack the prosecution's contention that Jerry Brudos could not have had the strength to carry a weighted body from his station wagon to the bridge rail over the Long Tom River—that *two* people would have had to be present to carry out such a feat.

The combined weight of Karen Sprinker's body and the engine head had been 179 pounds, the weight of an average man. A deadweight. In this context, a macabre term.

Burt called a private investigator who had been hired by the defense to carry out witnessed experiments, and introduced photographs showing that a station wagon like the Brudos' could be backed to within four inches of the bridge rail over the Long Tom.

"Did you carry a weight—weighing 179 pounds—from that station wagon to the bridge rail?" Burt asked the detective.

"I did, several times."

"Without assistance from another person?"

"No, sir. I carried the weight alone."

The jury had heard that Jerry Brudos was strong enough to hold back the weight of a freezer weighing between three and four hundred pounds. It seemed clear that he could have handled a weighted body with some ease.

The defense rested its case.

But District Attorney Gortmaker had something more, something to bring back on rebuttal.

The nude pictures of Darcie Brudos.

Long before, Darcie had feared that technicians in a photo lab might have seen some of the pictures Jerry had taken of her. He had promised her that he had destroyed all those photos. But he had not. He had hoarded them, just as he'd kept all of his other pictures. Now they were introduced into evidence, and Darcie was humiliated to see them passed down the rows of jurors. Her nakedness exposed to the people who would judge her.

Gortmaker pointed out that Darcie wore high patent-leather pumps in the photos—pumps that seemed identical to those apparent in the pictures of Karen Sprinker. It had been such a long time ago. She had not remembered those shoes.

She felt the jury looking at her—glancing at the pictures of her naked body, posing for what she had thought were totally private photos.

Now it looked as if she had lied about the shoes. She had told the district attorney that she did not recognize any of the shoes recovered in the search of Jerry's workshop. But they were there on her own feet in the dozens of slides and photos. She had told the truth as she remembered it.

She had not lied—but it looked as if she had.

The time had come for final arguments. Whichever way it went, the ordeal of the trial was almost over.

On Thursday, October 2, Gary Gortmaker spoke for the prosecution. Darcie heard herself portrayed as a monstrous woman, a woman who had willingly helped her husband torture and kill a helpless girl. A woman who had then accompanied her husband when he disposed of the body. She was depicted as morally loose, someone who posed for photographs that verged on pornographic. She listened, and thought that the D.A. might well be talking about another woman entirely, someone she had never met—and certainly someone she herself would despise.

And she felt trickles of hate aimed from somewhere behind her, and knew. There were those in the gallery who still believed that she was guilty of all these things.

Mr. Burt had told her that each side would have to pull out all the stops, that she must let the legal rhetoric wash over her and not heed it, not allow it to damage her.

But it did.

The words would not wash over her; instead, they penetrated her fragile facade like acid eroding whatever self-esteem she had left. She would never escape them, no matter how far she went. She thought of the little childhood rhyme: "Sticks and stones . . . but words will never hurt me."

And all she could think of was how much words could hurt.

When it was over, Charlie Burt rose and walked to the jury rail.

"Lizzie Borden took an ax,
and gave her father forty whacks.
And when she saw what she had done,
She gave her mother forty-one. . . ."

The poem hung on the air.

"Lizzie Borden was acquitted of both those murders, ladies and gentlemen. Everyone connected with that old case is long dead—the judge, the jury, the lawyers, the defendant. Yet the poem remains—known to every schoolchild. *Why?* Because the public seizes upon the gruesome and the bizarre. Lizzie Borden has been convicted of those crimes by history and folklore."

Burt did not have to equate Jerome Henry Brudos' crimes with the horror of the Borden massacre. It was obvious; there had never been a more gruesome crime in Oregon crime annals than those committed by Jerry Brudos. Burt reminded the jury of the terrible photographs of Brudos' victims, photographs that could not help but revolt anyone who gazed upon them.

"Does the state want the truth . . . or does the state want a conviction? Is Darcie Brudos being prosecuted . . . or is she being persecuted? She was married—is *still* married—to this man. Does that automatically make her guilty by association?"

Burt pointed out again that Darcie had preserved evidence. He took the picture of Jerry Brudos simpering in the black lace slip and handed it to the jury. He took the other picture—the worst picture—of Jerry Brudos staring at his victim's hanging corpse, and held it out for them to see again.

"This is the face of a madman—a monster who inadvertently took his own picture. Do not convict Darcie Brudos because she is *married* to a madman.

"Take Edna Beecham out of the case . . . and it crumbles like a house of cards. If you *believe* Edna Beecham, *convict*. If you do not, *acquit*."

It was 4:09 P.M. on that bleak October afternoon when Judge Hay finished giving his final instructions and the jury retired to debate their verdict.

Darcie was returned to her jail cell to wait. Charlie Burt had told her it might be hours—or it might be days before the jury signaled that they had made their judgment.

The jail matrons were kind to her; they had always been kind to her. Now they brought her two aspirin and a glass of milk. She had never taken tranquilizers, and she would not now. But she was afraid—more afraid than she had been throughout the trial. There were no more words to be said. Whatever would be would be.

Five o'clock. Six o'clock.

At 7:59 P.M. she heard a matron approaching her cell, and she looked up.

"The jury's back. They're waiting for you."

Judge Hay turned to the jury foreman. "Have you reached a verdict?"

"We have, your Honor."

"And how do you find?"

Darcie tried to control her trembling as she faced the jury. She could not read their faces.

"*Not guilty.*"

— 23 —

In the Oregon State Penitentiary, Prisoner 33284 was now dealing with his peers. No, that would be a faulty term; Jerry Brudos' fellow prisoners would never accept him as one of their kind. They were not constrained by the law as the detectives, lawyers, and prosecutors had been. Despite his protestations that he had been treated badly after his arrest, he had been treated with eminent fairness.

Now he was in prison.

There are social hierarchies in prison that are just as clearly defined or even *more* clearly defined than those in other communities. The vast majority of prisoners are basically decent men who have, admittedly, broken laws—but who believe in the sanctity of human life and in the protection of women and children. The upper echelons in prison society are reserved for the "brains"—the safecrackers who can "see" with their fingers, the crafty con men, the bunco artists who are charming and devious and who can sweet-talk anyone out of anything, and, of course, the "paperhangers," the forgers and counterfeiters.

Brains count inside the walls; the smart cons are the jailhouse lawyers who can give advice on how to get out, or at least how to maneuver for favors inside. They are the elite.

Jerry Brudos was smart, but his crimes had been such that they obliterated any claim he might have had to join those respected for their intelligence.

The social ladder in the joint works on down, then, based on abilities that have no meaning in the outside world. Bank robbers are considered clever if they have managed to get away with a few such crimes before

they were apprehended. Burglars are above robbers—
"cat burglars" getting the nod. Sheer physical strength
is important. If you have no important contacts on the
outside, and you're not that brilliant, you can dominate in prison just by being muscular.

Close to the bottom are the penny-ante crooks. But
at the very, very bottom, according to the general
prison population, are the sex criminals. The rapists.
The child molesters.

And the woman killers.

Cons have women and children whom they love.
And as much as they love their own, they detest the
sex killer. If he did what he did to his victims, he
would be capable of doing the same to their women
and children.

The grapevine at Oregon State Prison had telegraphed
that Jerry Brudos was coming in, whispered intelligence that works faster than anything on the outside.

They were ready for him.

A sex killer on the inside is lucky if he only gets the
silent treatment. He must always be looking over his
shoulder, be aware that whatever punishment he managed to avoid in society may well be waiting for him.

He may lose his mind, or his balls, or his life in
prison.

There is a rule of thumb in prison: never put a
woman-killer in a cell on one of the upper tiers. He
may have an "accidental" fall. Jerry Brudos was housed
in a ground-floor cell.

The cons gave Jerry the silent treatment, declaring
him a nonperson.

When he moved through the chow lines, he kept his
eyes on his tray—watching the piles of starchy stuff for
which he had no appetite. Eating meant that he would
have to find a spot at one of the tables in the vast hall.

It didn't really matter where Jerry Brudos chose a
seat; he would be eating alone within a few moments.
Some one of the other prisoners would give a slight
nod, and the cons would get up en masse and move. It
was an effective way to ostracize him. All the other
tables would be crowded, and Jerry Brudos would be

left sitting alone at a long table, as visible as if a spotlight shone on him.

Jerry Brudos lost his appetite.

The prisoner was no longer overweight. Within a short time his weight had dropped to 150 pounds. Feeling the eyes of his fellow prisoners, hearing their comments directed at him—"Something stinks, I think I'm gonna puke"; "I don't eat with no perverts"; and "Woman killer"—he could only swirl his food around his plate and wait for the bell to clang.

Before—outside—he had had so much control over people; his strength made him respected. His flaring temper frightened them. Now, no one would even talk to him, and Darcie no longer wrote to him. He listened, always, for the sound of footsteps behind him.

On August 13, 1969, someone slammed a bucket of water into the left side of his head. His ears rang from the blow, and he was hustled off to the infirmary. Doctors there found he had a mild inflammation of the eardrum, but no perforation. He complained of pain in his lower back after the incident and was taken "outside" for a visit to a chiropractor.

He was positive that they were out to get him, that somebody—maybe the whole lot of them—only waited for the opportunity to kill him. He began to keep a log recording the dates and details of crimes against him.

He also began to study lawbooks available to him in prison, confident that he would find a way to get out through his intelligence and a clever use of legal procedure.

He did not repent his crimes or grieve for his victims. He only continued to rail at the unfairness of the whole situation.

Jerry Brudos objected to a great many things. He was furious that his children had been removed from him, insisting that he *was* a fit parent, and deserved a hearing. Darcie divorced him in August 1970, changed her name, and moved away. This, too, he found unfair. He had been a good husband, and now she had deserted him. Darcie and the youngsters were together again, and she would spend the years ahead trying to

forget Jerry Brudos and what he had done. Grateful to
Charlie Burt, Darcie would write to him from wherever she was—letters at first, and finally only a re-
membrance at Christmas. The name she chose for
herself and the children is a common name, and there
is nothing to be gained from revealing it here. She
seeks only anonymity and peace after horror.

Jerry began peppering the Oregon court system with
requests and writs, documents which he wrote pain-
stakingly in his own printed hand, following forms he
found in lawbooks. His spelling was often flawed, but
a faithful reproduction of his arguments tells much
about the man's thinking processes.

On September 18, 1970, Brudos submitted a petition for a "Writ of Mandanus, Before the Honorabe
Supreme Court of the State of Oregon." He listed
"exhibits" in his index, and began his seven-page argument:

Now comes the defendant/petitioner, Jerome
H. Brudos, who does at this time enter before
this Honorable Court, to issue a writ of Mandanus,
directed to the Marion County Circuit Court,
that NO later than the 15th day of October, 1970,
to:
1. Issue to the defendant/petitioner, a complete, exacting and Itemized reciept, particulary
describing each and every Iten removed from the
defendans posession by the Marion County Sheriff's Department, the Marion County District Attorney's Office, the Salem City Policce Department, and Any and ALL other oriznations who
did remove any or all property from the defendant's/petitioner's House, Garage, Outbuildings,
Automobiles, and ALL other containers, On,
About or After the 25th day of May, 1962 [sic].
2. To order dismissed and declair for Naught,
the Judgment for the apparent amount of $8,179.00
against the defendant for totaly unsubstaincated
and unfounded 'Costs and Disburshments,' against
him.
3. To release immediatly all property Not Taken

Upon a Serchwarrent, to the defendant/petitioner and his agent, one Ned Rawls . . .

—/OR/—

To order immediatly, a Jury trial as is guarnteed by the 6th or 7th Amendment of the United States Constitution, which ever shall apply, Also Artcle I, Section II or, Section 17 which ever shall apply.

Brudos then listed seventeen "authorities" he had gleaned from his research. He had forgotten the year of his crimes, listing instead 1962, but he had what he considered powerful arguments on his behalf:

—Presentment—
As can be seen from exibit 1, the Marion County Circuit Court has apparently given Judgment against the defendant/petitioner, yet the Court has ignored every inquirey, petition and ALL Requeats for information by this defendant/petitioner. This is such an obvious and flagrent, willful Violation of Constitutional Rights that it goes with [sic] saying, However, since this Court is not familiar with this case, this petitioner will attempt to lay out the full parimiters of the Case without the aid of an Attorney for the defendant/petitioner is without funds with which to employ an attorney.

There is no room for argument for the defendant/petioner has repeadly writen to the Marion County Circuit Court, the Marion District Attorney's Office seeking information and/or/ a reciept and yet nether office has responded once with so much as an acknowlegiment of reciept of the Letters, Let alone supplied any of the requested information conserning These matters.

The 5th and 14th Amendment to the United States Constitution, along with Article 1, Section(s) 10 ALL Guarntee "Due Process," but, Article 1, Section 20 goes on to guarntee that

"No Court shall be secret, but Justice shall be administered openly and without purchase," yet as was seen in exibit 1, That is the only notice the defendant/petitioner, has received and then that was quite by accident out of an old newspaper, and that was after the Judgment was given. The defendant's property was confiscated, the defendent sued, Judgment given, and then a second hearing held which Judgment was given that the defendant/petitioner has no claim upon his own personal property inspite of O.R.S. 23.160 and 23.200.

What was Jerry Brudos so angry about? The state of Oregon has seized his belongings, the tools and gear in his shop, in an attempt to repay the state some of the $8,000-plus that his court costs had totaled. To Jerry Brudos, the law was there to protect him. *And only him.*

To state that this Law is being used indiscrimitly would be so crass and Grossly incorrect for the facts are plain and simple, This law has been used very discrimitly and soley against the defendant/petitioner. . . .

He cited two pages of statutes that he felt applied to himself, and then railed at the court:

Well it goes without saying that if we convict a man of a crime, place him in jail and then stand idely by while His tools of his trade and personal property stolden systematicly and Legaly? We then must have reformed him even if He must turn to a Life of Crime for he no longer has the needed tools with which to work at his ocupation or proper clothing Etc. This further only dimenstrats the Marion County Court Attitude Twards Justice. They don't give a damn about the Laws, Constitution or anything else except, they have a helpless victim who cannot fight Back and Two Court appointed attorneys who will co-operate with the Court or the prosecution's Lest Whim.

*   *   *

A Freudian slip? Or only the man's view of *himself* as a "helpless victim who cannot fight back"?

Judge Val Sloper had taken exquisite pains to be sure that Jerry Brudos had understood what he was pleading guilty to—but a year in prison had clouded Brudos' memory. Now he was claiming complete innocence of the crimes.

> During the arguments before the Court of Appeals [sic] upon another facit of this case, it was broght out that the Circuit Court Judge ordered the defendant's attorneys to Look at the psudo evidence compiled. That was on a Friday and the defendant was to go to trial the following monday and yet One attorney had not even bothered to look at the evidence. When the defendant requested to see the evidence he was told by his Attorneys "Oh no you don't get to see the evidence." The defendant has since found out why. There is photographs that were manifactured to make it appear Like the defendant was guilty of the Crime and the prosecution could not afford to Allow the defendant to see these phony pictures. They then proceeded to Threatnen the defendant's Life along with repurcussions which would be effected upon his wife and children.
>
> Marion County in That respect makes the Communiust Countrys and their methods Look Like Mickey Mouse Culb, for the defendant has the prrof and yet the Marion County Courts are concerned about a conviction only and could care Less that the Victim of this whole thing is in fact innosent. It can be seen from Exibit 2, Clearly shows that this is in fact the truth yet everybody says, "I sincerely doubt that it happened," yet nobody bothered to check. A plain and simple fact. There is a multitude of witnesses and evidence to substaciate this along with his personal testimony.

Brudos' "Exibit 2" was a statement purportedly made by a fellow prisoner alleging that Brudos had been treated unfairly, and repeating Brudos' feeling that he had been poisoned in jail! The statement mentioned that Brudos' bedding had been removed during the day and returned only at night. Since the prisoner had threatened suicide, it was a prudent move on the part of the jail staff. Brudos *was* fed separately from the other prisoners; it was for his own protection. In the Marion County jail, there might well have been other inmates who would have delighted in poisoning him, if the opportunity arose. It was hardly information that was new to the courts. Nor was it a legally sound basis for a new trial.

Brudos wound up his "mandanus" writ with an emotional paragraph:

The really teriable part is that the defendant/petitioner is in fact innocent of The Charges, yet the prosecution did have such a Lever against the defendant they got confessions for Cases that they didn't even have boddies for. Such threats were used that they could obtain such confessions yet the defense attorneys did not even question that. If One Court, Just One would have retained It's impartiality and had attempted to seek the truth and Justice it whould have been exposed, but Marion County Judicial system is so far out upon a Limb they fear of sawing it off Them self, there fore "we" says the Court "Will do nothing without an order stating we must, then we will have to try to get around that then."

The petitioner/defendant does therefore pray this Honorable Court will issue this writ of Mandanus and start to instill some form of Justice in the County that the State Capitol is in and this type of Decay can only spreed if not checked now.

Did Jerry Brudos believe his own arguments? Perhaps.

Perhaps he only wanted out.

The "confessions" had been made by Brudos himself. Yes, he had confessed to killing Linda Slawson and Jan Whitney, knowing that their bodies had not been found. He had chosen to brag about the murders to Jim Stovall.

In the late summer of 1970, the lack of those victims' bodies was a moot point—at least in the case of Jan Whitney. Picnickers along the Willamette River at a spot somewhat below the Independence Bridge saw what they took to be a lamb's carcass caught up in branches near the shore.

It was not a lamb; it was all that was left of Jan Whitney, her body surfacing so many months after she had had the terrible misfortune of meeting Jerome Henry Brudos. Identification was possible only through dental records. Cause of death could no longer be determined.

Brudos was a frequent patient in the prison infirmary. The records are cryptic, and give no details.

On January 1, 1971, he was treated for "rectal bleeding." Perhaps he suffered from hemorrhoids; possibly there were other reasons.

He had lost his battle to recover his property so that he might carry on his occupation. Since he was serving three life terms back-to-back, it was doubtful that his services as an electrician would be soon available to citizens in the Salem area.

A small ad appeared in the Salem *Capital Journal* and the Salem *Statesman* on March 23, 1971:

> Sheriff's Sale—March 27, 1971, 1 P.M. Marion County Shops, 5155 Silverton Rd. N.E., Craftsman Roll Cabinet and Tools, Electric Hand Tools, Rifle Re-Loading Equipment, Antique Telephone Insulators, Scuba Diving Equipment, Many Miscellaneous Items. Terms: Cash.

Sales were brisk. The gear taken from Jerry Brudos' grisly workshop netted the state of Oregon something over eleven hundred dollars. The citizens of the state would have to pay for the rest of Jerry Brudos' legal procedures through their taxes.

There were others who attempted to obtain Jerry

Brudos' property. His mother, Eileen, asserted that it was all rightfully hers—since she had lent him so much money, by her own reckoning—that had never been repaid. Ned Rawls and another friend asked for some of Brudos' tools and guns, and Darcie too laid claim to the gear left behind.

All of them were denied. Darcie's claims against the estate had already been satisfied when she signed a receipt for certain items: a movie screen, a camera, lawn chairs, throw rugs not used in evidence, a box fan, two blankets, a box of slides, miscellaneous personal papers, and a BB gun.

These were to be her assets, along with some furniture and clothes—very little after eight years of marriage.

Jerry Brudos continued to suffer "accidents" in prison. In 1971 his neck was broken, fractured at the fifth cervical bone, "C-5." He refused to say just how it had been broken, and it is not explained in his medical records beyond the terse "Fracture at C-5. Patient placed in body cast, healed in an acceptable position."

Brudos frequently complained of migraine headaches, palpitations, depression, and myriad other symptoms. He was treated with Meritene and Ritalin and various combinations of drugs to alleviate his headaches.

He remained a pariah among his fellow prisoners.

He kept up his filing of notices of appeal. In 1972 the basis of his appeal was bizarre; he contended that the dead girl in one picture was not Karen Sprinker at all (detectives had asked Dr. Sprinker to look only at the facial portion of the picture to save him further pain). Brudos said he had been convicted for killing someone unknown. With almost unthinkable gall, Brudos wanted to subpoena Karen Sprinker's father. He wanted to force Dr. Sprinker to study the grotesque pictures of his daughter, and then he submitted that he, Brudos, could prove that the girl portrayed was not Karen, but a stranger, a woman who was a willing subject he'd photographed years before!

Blessedly for the grieving family, the appeal was denied.

By December 1974 Jerry Brudos had seized upon an entirely new theory, a theory somewhat supported by a psychologist he had been seeing in prison. Brudos had always avoided any responsibility for his crimes; now he had a handle on something that he felt would explain all of it. The psychologist had suggested that Brudos was hypoglycemic. That is, that he had low blood sugar, a condition blamed—rightly or wrongly—for many of modern man's physical and emotional problems.

Not all the prison psychological staff agreed with the diagnosis of hypoglycemia, however. In an evaluation done on December 11, 1974, one doctor wrote of Brudos:

I see Mr. Brudos as a paranoid personality without any real evidence of thought disorder or a psychotic process. He is able to conform his behavior to his environment, and is functioning very efficiently and without difficulty. He is quite an intelligent individual, and, coupled with his paranoia, he is a problem in management. He had a very good relationship in therapy with Dr. B., but the benefit of this relationship was that Dr. B. thought the basic difficulty was that of a physical disease—mainly hypoglycemia. And in this way, Mr. Brudos could escape the responsibility for the heinous crimes. With the present mental status of Mr. Brudos, I see him as a potentially very dangerous individual were he to be released into the community. This situation will continue unless he has intensive and prolonged psychotherapy—not group therapy—but at the present time this does not seem realistic with the shortage of available trained personnel. I strongly recommend there be no change in the current situation concerning Mr. Brudos.

Brudos would not let go of the "hypoglycemic" diagnosis; he saw it as his ticket out of prison and his vindication. In a hearing in October 1976 he submitted this theory to the court. He had "fired" a succession of court-appointed attorneys, but his new lawyer asked for time so that famed Dr. Lendon Smith, "The Children's Doctor" of television note, could submit a letter on his evaluation of Jerry Brudos' condition.

Smith is highly respected in the pediatric field, a man of great humor and skill. Surprisingly to those who watch him on television, he also has a background in working with psychotic prisoners and soldiers as a psychiatrist in the late forties. He espouses the theory that poor nutrition often contributes to antisocial behavior.

Smith wrote on November 1, 1976:

> . . . Violence, headaches, drowsiness, allergies, hyperactivity, irrational and even psychotic behavior may all be due to low blood sugar; the thinking part of the brain simply cannot respond rationally to the environment when it is deprived of energy.
>
> There is no doubt that Mr. Brudos had hypoglycemia in 1973. The log of his daily jail activities can allow for no doubt that he was hypoglycemic in June 1969. People have a potential or proclivity to hypoglycemia and they will become hypoglycemic when their diet is rich in carbohydrate. I am aware of the high-carbohydrate diet in prisons.
>
> I am sure his hypoglycemia was activated by the diet he received in jail in June 1969.

And so Jerry Brudos now blamed all of his crimes—if he should admit guilt—and his confession in June, 1969 on a diet too high in carbohydrates and sugar!

The appeals court took a dim view of the "too many candy bars and mashed potatoes" theory. Jerry Brudos remained in prison.

In toto, 1976 had not been Brudos' best year. Darcie had obtained an order forbidding her children to visit their father in prison, nor did she want them to correspond with him. She was still afraid of him—for herself, and especially for the children's emotional well-being.

Jerry had also lost his phone privileges—after still another extended hearing. A female employee in the warden's office reported that Brudos had phoned her and told her that "she was cute," instructing her to come to a window so that he could see her better. When this was documented, the prisoner's access to the phone was taken away.

Jerry was becoming angry . . . and frightened. He felt always that someone stalked him, someone inside the prison. His fellow cons had never warmed to him. He had regained the weight he'd lost initially, but he sensed the hatred all around him. He complained, "Sometimes, it appears as though the penitentiary is just bent on trying point-blankly to get me killed."

Not the penitentiary staff certainly. Whatever their private feelings, their mandate was only to keep Brudos away from the public. The prisoners themselves? That was another matter entirely.

The last appeal of record filed in the Oregon State Supreme Court's dusty archives notes the date: May 25, 1977. By 1977, several infamous serial killers had emerged to replace Jerry Brudos in the headlines. Ted Bundy had allegedly murdered young women in Washington, Oregon, Utah, and Colorado, and was currently in the Utah State Prison. In the same prison at Point of the Mountain, Gary Gilmore had faced a firing squad, but only after generating enough newsprint to encircle the world if placed end to end. There was Juan Corona in California. Crime was in the news, and television talk shows were rife with discussions of the efficacy of the death penalty.

Jerry Brudos based this last appeal on a rather convoluted theory. Since *his* alleged crimes were so heinous, and since one of his own attorneys had once compared his crimes to those of Jack the Ripper and the Boston Strangler, he now put forth the premise that media coverage equated recent heinous and sensational crimes with his own. His paranoia had expanded. While he had formerly felt that the prison staff and population were against him, he now insisted that the entire state of Oregon was plotting against him, and that his life was in danger. His next point seemed diametrically opposed to his protestations that he feared for his life. "The extraordinary security measures taken to protect me in prison make the courts unable to be objective on my appeals . . ."

And he reiterated that his hypoglycemic condition in 1969 had made him unable to plead with a clear and unconfused mind.

Again, Jerry Brudos was denied a new trial.

Outside, the world has gone on without Jerry Brudos. His mother, Eileen Brudos, the mother he claimed to detest, died in 1971. Darcie Brudos has a new name and a new life. Her children are almost grown now. The Sprinkers, the Salees, the Slawsons, and the Whitneys have picked up the pieces of their shattered lives. Lt. Gene Daugherty rose to the position of Deputy Superintendent of the Oregon State Police before his retirement in 1980. Jim Stovall is a lieutenant now in charge of Patrol units for the Salem police department.

The horror has diminished with the passage of time, but will never fade entirely.

Afterword

March 1, 1988

Will Jerome Henry Brudos ever get out of prison? The rational answer is no. However, an overview of "lifers" who *have* been released on parole after ten or twelve or fourteen years is not reassuring. In the vast majority of states in America, "life in prison" means somewhere between ten and fourteen years. "Good behavior" generally cuts sentences by a third. In Oregon, a convicted killer can technically apply for parole in six months. While parole has never been granted so soon, most convicted killers in Oregon are back on the streets within a dozen years.

One Portland man, convicted in the early sixties in the mutilation murder of a housewife, served a little over twelve years in the Oregon State Prison in Salem. During his "life" sentence, he was trained to be an apprentice plumber. He was a model prisoner—as most sadistic sociopaths are. Within a month of his parole, he repeated his crime, using an identical M.O. (Modus Operandi). He was arrested for killing and dismembering a woman he met in a bar, although detectives believe his actual new toll is three victims, not one.

The same thing happened with an Oregon City murderer who was released in the late seventies and went to work as a school janitor. He was subsequently arrested and convicted of killing the high school teacher whom he had dated until she discovered his criminal record. When she confronted him, and threatened to tell school authorities, he killed her.

Oregon is no worse than any other state. It is only representative of a profoundly dangerous problem, and this book happens to be about a killer who operated in

Oregon. Prisoners convicted of heinous crimes are released every day in every state *years* before their sentence release date. In some cases, their prison records have been exemplary. In others, infraction slips have mysteriously disappeared before they ever reached the hands of the parole board.

There are many reasons for parole to occur so much earlier than the layman might expect. Prisons are full to bursting, and the cost of keeping one prisoner in a penitentiary for just one year ranges from $6,000 to $15,000. "Old" crimes tend to be forgotten, buried under the mountains of media coverage of new crimes that mount up inexorably year after year. A man whose name has been infamous becomes just another number after he has been in prison for two decades. He becomes a "nobody" in the world of crime.

And sometimes he gets out. *Often*, he gets out. So many killers slip through the cracks of the justice system; only the hue and cry of the media or victims' support groups serves to remind parole boards, prison administrators, and legislators of the crimes that sent him to prison for "life."

Jerome Brudos. Is it possible that he too may one day convince a parole board in Oregon that he is safe to be at large?

Quite.

That possibility is the impetus behind this book. The "monster" may sleep, but he only slumbers—waiting for his chance to roam free once more. He does not get better. There is no psychiatric treatment today that cures a sadistic sociopath. Minor behavior modification is the most studies have been able to promise, and that modification usually disappears when active treatment ceases.

Jerry Brudos had been in the Oregon State Penitentiary for almost twenty years. He has changed little in appearance in those two decades. He has long since regained the weight he lost in his first months in prison, and he is once again a bulky, lumbering giant of a man. He is still freckled, but his hair is much thinner, and the blond is considerably grayed. He is forty-nine years old now.

There is an old saying among convicts: No matter how long your sentence, you only do "hard time" for one year. The literal translation is that human beings acclimate. Prison becomes a little world.

Jerry Brudos has acclimated. Since prison mail is not censored in Oregon, he is able to pursue his overweening interest. He sends away for—and receives—every catalog he can find featuring, of course, women's shoes. He stacks them up in the corner of his cell for slow perusal and study.

He earns spending money by making leather key fobs. He always liked the touch of leather. Over the years, he has probably turned out hundreds of the key rings stamped with jobs, hobbies, avocations, college logos, and mascots. Prison visitors who choose to can pay a dollar or two for a slightly ghoulish souvenir. A whole display board is filled with leather key fobs that Jerry Brudos once touched and shaped.

The tags read "Jerry Brudos—Box 33284."

Today, with the evolution of electronics into a world that Brudos could only have imagined twenty years ago, he has become totally involved with computers. The man whose writing seems to be that of a near illiterate remains a genius with electronics. The Oregon State Penitentiary has a network of computers and word processors and who would be more adept at keeping them humming than Jerry Brudos? Some informants insist he "runs the whole prison computer system," and others deem him only a technician who helps out.

Were it not for his fetishes and his fantasies, for his obsession with death, Jerry Brudos—on the outside—could probably have made a fortune working with computers.

But, in the end, murder became paramount to Jerry Brudos. To the layman, a killer is a killer is a killer. To the criminologist, there are as many gradations of the violence in murder as there are colors in the rainbow. Humans kill for financial gain. Humans kill because of jealousy. Humans kill one another for revenge or out of fear or even to achieve a kind of infamy. But the lust killer, the sadistic killer, the serial killer, is a breed unto himself.

Little Jerry Brudos, the five-year-old who was transfixed by a pair of women's shoes, and who then evolved through so-called "minor" sex crimes over thirty years to commit multiple murders fits the majority of the guidelines established for the lust killer/serial killer. It is a category which Jerry Brudos resents mightily. He threatened to sue an Oregon newspaper for deeming him a "lust killer." "I'm a killer, yes," he wrote. "But I'm not a *lust killer*." A matter of pride . . . or semantics? (Brudos withdrew his suit when he was reminded of his psychiatric report.)

Because the number of these murderers has grown alarmingly in America since the early 1960s, the Behavioral Science Unit of the F.B.I. carries on continual research to update our knowledge of them.

During the black years when the big man with the friendly, almost-shy grin acted out his secret fantasies, there was no definitive term to describe his psychopathology. The phrase "serial killer" had yet to be coined. In the 1960s, the press lumped his kind of killer in with all the others who murdered many victims. "Mass murderers" they were deemed. But this freckled giant was not a mass murderer, nor was Albert De Salvo, "The Boston Strangler," whose crimes had taken place 3000 miles away and half a decade earlier. Nor was Jack-the-Ripper a mass murderer as he prowled night after night through the narrow streets of London's red-light district.

They were all serial killers, men who killed their victims one at a time over a long time—men who would never stop until they were arrested or too old—or dead.

How far back in criminal history can we trace serial killers? Possibly to the very beginning. Bob Ressler, of the F.B.I.'s Behavioral Science Unit, suggests that the werewolves of gypsy fables were, in actuality, not murderous mutants at all, but serial killers. Humans, after all, but as deadly as werewolves.

By 1988, the term "serial killer" would be well

known, these killers-by-the-numbers a favorite topic of talk shows, and the concern of law enforcement officials all over America. These are the men who stalk and kill and wait . . . and stalk and kill again and wait.

Jerry Brudos was one of them. Twenty years ago, this man with the broad bland face was as dangerous and deadly as any murderer since time began. But, in 1968, he was tragically ahead of his time. For a long time no one knew he was out there, scheming and trolling for victims.

Even when they found him, he was difficult to categorize. Today, the Jerome Henry Brudos case is used by criminologists, detectives, professors, psychologists, and psychiatrists as one of the classic examples of murderous horror. Infamous, Brudos is nevertheless sought out by experts who would interview him, seeking some way to untangle the bloody threads of his life. He is not only a serial killer; he is a lust killer.

The worst of the worst.

Special Agents R. Roy Hazelwood and John E. Douglas have isolated the profile of this most dreaded killer in their paper "The Lust Murderer."

They might well have been describing Jerome Henry Brudos.

Basically, there are two types of personalities, who commit lust murders: the Organized Nonsocial and Disorganized Asocial (and occasionally, one who possesses characteristics of both). Jerry Brudos' personality fits into the parameters of the first type easily. According to Hazelwood and Douglas, the Organized Nonsocial killer is a person who is completely heedless of the welfare of society; he cares only for himself. Other humans matter *only* in the ways they fulfill—or deny—his needs. While he dislikes other people, he does not avoid them. Rather, he shows the rest of the world an amiable facade. It allows him to manipulate them toward his own goals. He is quite cunning, and he plans well.

The lust killer is a man full of fantasy—Brudos, for example, drew pictures in his mind of the "killing place" where he could imprison captive women, torture them, and then freeze them for his pleasure forever. He was fascinated early on with pornography, and used it to build on his own fantasies. Psychiatrists detect a glaring lack of self-confidence in the lust killer. Like Brudos, he can ward off reality by sinking into his cruel fantasies. Therein lies his power over all the women who have rejected him.

For Brudos, the first rejection by a woman is easy to pinpoint: his own mother did not like him. He could never please her in any way.

The true lust killer finds his victims because they come to him. That is, they *cross his path*. He does not choose them ahead of the killing time, but he is always ready. Linda Slawson came to Jerry Brudos' home to sell encyclopedias. Although she had gone to the wrong address, for *him* it was propitious. Jan Whitney's car had broken down on the freeway just moments before Brudos passed by on his way home from work. Karen Sprinker had the misfortune to be in the parking garage of a department store while Brudos was seeking another woman, a woman who had evaded him. And Linda Salee too walked out of a busy store at the most dangerous moment—only to meet Jerry Brudos.

Until the terrible moment when they became his choice, he had never seen any of them before. . . .

They had crossed his path.

The motivations behind the commission of a lust murder are emotions alien to a normal male. The lust killer is a sadist for whom sex and cruelty are so interwoven that, for him, one does not exist without the other. Although he may deny interest in sex when he is arrested, it is quite probably the most intense stimulus in his life. The victim is not a real person to him. Indeed, there *are* no other *real* people in his life. Only himself. His victim is only a vehicle for his own pleasure.

Jerry Brudos has told psychiatrists that, once he began his attacks, there was never any thought of not carrying through. He killed under the influence of an urge that even he himself could not—cannot—define. It was something that was to be done. His victims had been drawn into the fantasies that had become reality to him.

Because Jerry Brudos was really a most inadequate man, a "Casper Milquetoast" among other men, he needed to demean and possess women. He could not seem to possess Darcie, as hard as he tried to control her. She was slipping away from him—at least in his own mind. But he could possess his love-hate objects: women. He could trap them, torture them, confine them, and eventually destroy them. When he did that, his anxiety was assuaged for a time. In Brudos' case, the time seemed to be about a month. Just as Jim Stovall had predicted, Brudos prowled under a pseudo-menstrual cycle.

The lust killer's modus operandi is marked by brutality and sadism, say Hazelwood and Douglas. Invariably the victim's bodies are mutilated, and mutilated in areas that have sexual connotation: the genitals, the breasts, the buttocks. Brudos' fixation was on the breasts; he destroyed them by literally cutting them away from the dead victims.

It is rare for a lust killer to shoot his victims; he requires the direct contact of beating, strangulation, or stabbing. Jerry Brudos used the leather postal strap and his hanging device. As with other lust killers, the main portion of his sexual attack occurred while his victims were unconscious or dead. His innate fear of female rejection continued to such a degree that, even when his victims were helplessly bound, he could not risk their fighting him.

Most lust killers have a scenario that requires they take a souvenir of their killings. Here, too, Jerry Brudos worked in a pattern that was predictable. He saved shoes, undergarments, and photographs, and, exceeding even heretofore infamous lust killers, he saved the severed breasts and attempted to make paperweights out of them.

There is one characteristic common to most lust killers that may be surprising. They seem obsessed by driving, often driving hundreds of miles. They travel long distances trolling for victims, and Brudos was no exception. His battered station wagon was constantly on the I-5 freeway, going to Portland, back to Salem, then to Corvallis. This may be a manifestation of their anxiety, of the need to keep moving. More likely, it is their innate cunning that inspires this; they have learned that they will avoid detection more easily if they commit their crimes in widely separated police jurisdictions. They seek to have their "patterns" known only to themselves.

Agents Douglas and Hazelwood have determined that most lust killers are relatively young—between seventeen and twenty-five years of age. Brudos began his sexual crimes at the age of sixteen, but he managed to avoid serious consequences for his heinous crimes until he was thirty years old. In that way, he was, perhaps, cleverer than most, and in his perverted mind, he considered it something of an accomplishment. When he was finally face-to-face with Jim Stovall, he was eager to brag about his crimes.

Like all lust killers, Jerry Brudos was fascinated with the investigation. He saved newspaper clippings to gloat over, secure that he was smarter than the cops in this deadly game. He was alarmed when police investigated the hole left in his garage after the accident, and yet smug that they could have come so close and still not caught him. When Stovall questioned Brudos, it was Brudos who asked so eagerly, "How can you tell? How can you figure out that I did anything?"

He was still very confident at that point.

Jerry Brudos is Caucasian, and so were all his victims. It is almost unheard-of for a lust killer to cross racial lines. Since his hatred of women appears to stem from women in his own life—a mother, a wife, a sister—he tends to attack within his own race. The victims may resemble physically the women who have rejected him, or, as in Brudos' case, they may be the very antithesis. Eileen Brudos had always worn plain clothing, dull flat-heeled shoes, and little makeup. Her son grew up to kill pretty women who wore pretty clothing. Unlike Brudos, Ted Bundy, alleged to have murdered thirty-six young women, chose victims who were beautiful and who resembled the lost fiancée who had rejected him. Whether the lust killer chooses opposites or doubles for his hate object, he *does* invariably choose victims who fit his particular victim profile.

Few lust killers begin by actually murdering. It is a slow but constantly accelerating process—a juggernaut of perversion, if you will. Many begin with voyeurism: "Peeping Toms." Some are exposers. It is a fallacy that such offenses are not dangerous and will not progress. There is always the constant need for more stimulus, more excitement. Jerry Brudos began by stealing shoes, moving on to the theft of women's undergarments. He was a voyeur. When the theft of lingerie from clotheslines was not enough, he actually entered homes to steal his treasures. Here too was an added excitement. William Heirens, the seventeen-year-old premed student convicted of the mutilation murder of six-year-old Suzanne Degnan in Chicago in the 1940s, and other sex killings, related to arresting officers that he achieved sexual climax only when he crossed over the windowsill of a home where he went to steal undergarments. That his crimes accelerated fatally is well-documented. (Heirens, over fifty today, is still in prison.)

Jerry Brudos found that the theft of shoes and bras and panties was not enough to fill the void in his self-esteem, not enough to quiet his anxiety and rage. And so he raped. When that was no longer enough, he killed and mutilated his victims.

And if he had not been caught . . . ?

The question must always be "Why?" What happens to change a chubby-cheeked, freckled five-year-old into a monster? If there were clearly definitive answers, it might be simpler to explain. But there are certain factors which seem to be present in the history of almost all lust killers.

With the complete records available on Jerry Brudos' past, the reader can easily see the correlations between his case and the accepted profile put together by experts.

Special agents Hazelwood and Douglas offer their opinion based on their studies of scores of cases:

What set of circumstances creates the individual who becomes the lust murderer? . . . It is generally accepted that the foundation of the personality is formed within the first few years of life. While extreme stress, frequent narcotic use, or alcohol abuse can cause personality disorganization in later life, it is the early years that are critical to the personality structure and development.

Seldom does the lust murder come from an environment of love and understanding. It is more likely that he was an abused or neglected child who experienced a great deal of conflict in his early life and was unable to develop and use adequate coping devices. Had he been able to do so, he would have withstood the stresses placed on him and developed normally in early childhood. . . .

These stresses, frustrations, and subsequent anxieties, along with the inability to cope with them, may lead the individual to withdraw from the society which he perceives as hostile and threatening. Through the internalization process, he becomes secluded and isolated from others. . . . This type possesses a poor self-image and secretly rejects the society which he feels rejects him.

Family and associates would describe him as a nice quiet person who keeps to himself, but who never quite realized his potential. During adolescence, he may have engaged in voyeuristic activities or the theft of feminine clothing. Such activities serve as a substitute for his inability to approach a woman sexually in a mature and confident manner.

The individual designated as the organized nonsocial type harbors similar feelings of hostility, but elects not to withdraw and internalize his hostility. Rather, he overtly expresses it through aggressive and seemingly senseless acts against society. Typically, he begins to demonstrate his hostility as he passes through puberty and into adolescence. He would be described as a troublemaker and manipulator of people, concerned only with himself. . . .

Jerry Brudos falls somewhere between the two types. He was a quiet youngster—as far as anyone knew—until his attacks on the two teenage girls, attacks which landed him in the Oregon State Hospital. Would adequate treatment at that time have worked? Perhaps. But he did not receive intensive treatment; he was viewed only as a sissy, lazy, and told he needed to grow up.

It is likely that it was far too late at that point anyway; his fantasies were already formed and they would never leave him.

Have they left him now? After eighteen years in prison? That too is extremely doubtful. The mold was formed so early. Like Kenneth Bianchi (the alleged "Hillside Strangler"), Edward Kemper (Northern California's "Chainsaw Murderer-Coed Killer"), and Wisconsin's infamous Edward Gein, Jerome Brudos is the product of a home with a strong, controlling mother, and with a weak (or absent) father figure (although these men cannot all be considered lust killers).

Jerry Brudos hates women. He has almost always hated women. And, in all likelihood, he will continue to hate women. Like Delilah's hold over Samson, women weaken Jerry Brudos and make him afraid. He can control them only by obliterating them.

Brudos and Bundy and Bianchi and Long and Kemper and the many others who came out of the shadows to kill, and who were finally caught, are in prison. There are other prowlers who are still free. There is virtually no way to spot this kind of danger until it strikes. Women can protect themselves by being constantly aware, by avoiding lonely places.

While there is no sure means of escaping from the control of the lust murderer, fighting him presents the only possible avenue of escape.

Fight. The lust killer is a coward who counts upon his chosen victim to be passive. If his quarry screams and kicks and fights, she may escape with her life.

But, if she allows him to take her away to his isolated killing place, thinking that she can reason with him, she will surely die.

Because he has no mercy in him.

No one who encountered Jerry Brudos has ever forgotten him. The detectives who tracked him and finally caught him will never forget him.

Jim Stovall rose to the rank of Lieutenant, and helped solve dozens of homicide cases long after Brudos was in prison. He retired from the Salem Police Department in the mid eighties, and divides his time between living and skiing in Colorado and his home in Salem. He still studies the criminal mind, and the ever-more-scientific methods devised to track and trap murderers.

Jerry Frazier moved from the Salem Police Department to the Marion County District Attorney's Office where he works as an investigator. Not too long ago, he found himself stopping in front of the *shake* house on Center Street. He talked to the current tenants, who admitted that they would never have moved in— had they known the house's history. No, there were no ghosts; it was just the idea.

"They had a lot of turnover of renters," Frazier recalls. "The place always had people moving in or moving out. That day, I walked into that garage after so many years. The dividers were gone, but the *feeling*—a kind of chill—was still there. Just as much as the day Jerry Brudos offered me that rope knot that was eventually going to help convict him."

In April of 1984, I was presenting a seminar to the Oregon Writers Colony at Gearhart, Oregon, on the Pacific Ocean. Using slides, I moved through the lives of the serial killers I had written about. When I had finished speaking, I looked up to see an attractive red-haired woman standing in front of me. If it is possible to be that color, she was pale gray-green. She looked, literally, as if she had seen a ghost.

"Are you all right?" I asked.

"I was the one . . . who got away," she murmured. "I was the one he called the 'blonde bitch.' "

"You're in my book," I said. " Have you read it?"

She shook her head. "After I got away, I found out that he was arrested for murder—but something stopped me from reading about it. I didn't want to know what he'd done. I didn't want to know how close I'd come . . . I guess I didn't want to know the details."

Understandable, after what she had been through. The woman was Sharon Wood, alive and well fifteen years after her terrifying few minutes with Jerry Brudos.

However, after our chance meeting in the lodge on the Oregon beach, Sharon Wood felt a pressing need to find out more about the man who had tried to destroy her life. She asked, as she had asked herself right after the attack, "Why am *I* alive . . . while the others are dead?"

She thought of her twins born in 1970, Dori and Christopher, children who would never have been born if she hadn't escaped from Jerry Brudos. And, in doing so, Sharon Wood could not help but think of the children that Karen Sprinker, Jan Whitney, Linda Slawson, and Linda Salee might have had. Of the years they might have had.

Wood, a free-lance writer and photographer herself by 1984, was compelled to learn more about Brudos— this man whose story she had avoided for so many years. She sent away to the Portland Police Department for the follow-up report on her own case, and she visited the Oregon State Penitentiary and interviewed the warden's assistant.

She found that the prison staff considered Jerry Brudos "a model prisoner," and that he was one of the small percentage allowed to work in the hobby shop. Sharon stood in front of the window displaying Brudos' key fobs, and she felt her spine tighten. One was stamped "Portland State Vikings": Portland State is the college where Brudos attacked her; and another was stamped with a camera.

Grateful that he had never had the opportunity to take his ghastly pictures of her, she paid one dollar and bought the leather fob with the camera on it.

Today, Sharon Wood works to help other women learn self-defense. She wholeheartedly supports the Portland Police Department's "Womenstrength" program. It is easy to see that Sharon feels an obligation to victims, and that she is grateful that she was allowed to live out her life.

Although Jerry Brudos is not likely to get out of prison until he is a very old man, there are other killers who thus far have avoided being newsworthy. They are just as dangerous—and they have never been caught; they are still prowling. Their philosophy on the value of a human life can be summed up, just as Jerry Brudos' was, in a short anecdote told by a detective who met him sometime after his arrest.

Jim Byrnes, a Marion County detective at the time of Brudos' arrest in 1969, and now a private investigator, recalls a conversation with Jerry Brudos.

"He liked strawberry milkshakes, and I'd take them to him to try to get him to talk. I wanted to get at how he really felt. One day, I asked him, 'Do you feel some remorse, Jerry? Do you feel sorry for your victims—for the girls who died?'

"There was a half piece of white paper on the table between us, and he picked it up, crumpled it in his fist, and threw the ball of paper on the floor. 'That much,' he said. 'I care about those girls as much as I care about that piece of wadded-up paper. . . .'"